AF560154

MICRO FINANCE AND WOMEN EMPOWERMENT

MICRO FINANCE AND WOMEN EMPOWERMENT

Edited by

Dr. G.Vijaya Bharathi

Assistant Professor

Dept. of Commerce

Yogi Vemana University

Kadapa–516 003

(India)

DISCOVERY PUBLISHING HOUSE PVT. LTD.

NEW DELHI-110 002

Published by:
Tilak Wasan
DISCOVERY PUBLISHING HOUSE PVT. LTD.
4383/4B, Ansari Road, Darya Ganj
New Delhi-110 002 (India)
Phone : +91-11-23279245, 43596064-65
Fax : +91-11-23253475
E-mail : parul.wasan@gmail.com
discoverypublishinghouse@gmail.com
web : www.discoverypublishinggroup.com

***First Edition:* 2012**

ISBN: 978-93-5056-105-8

Micro Finance and Women Empowerment

Printed at:
Shree Balaji Art Press
Delhi

Preface

Microfinance refers to small savings, credit and insurance services extended to socially and economically disadvantaged segments of the society. Microfinance is claimed to be powerful tool which can be used effectively to address poverty, empower the socially marginalized poor and strengthen the social fabric. Microfinance institutions are engaged in the provision of financial services to the poor. Microfinance is acting as potent tool in reducing the vulnerable situations of women. In India too, microfinance is making headway for reduction of poverty and empowering rural women. Women empowerment has gained considerable significance in the recent past as an area of policy interventions and initiatives. No country can achieve its potential without adequately investing in and developing the capabilities of women. Women empowerment is an active process of enabling women to realize their identity, potentiality and power in all spheres of their life. Microfinance as an innovative mechanism provided a variety of financial products and services helping women to build their businesses, families and communities. The challenges and opportunities provided to the women of digital era are growing rapidly that the job seekers are turning into job creators. They are flourishing as designers, interior decorators, exporters, publishers, garment manufacturers and what not, still exploring new avenues of economic participation. In India, although women constitute a majority of the population, efforts taken towards to strengthen women entrepreneurs could not reach the rural and backward areas due to major constraints like lack of confidence, socio-cultural barriers, market-oriented risks, motivational factors, knowledge in business administration, awareness about the financial assistance, etc. Hence there is an imperative need for improving the access of women to national resources for ensuring their equitable place in the mainstream of economic development. To elevate the status of women, they must be economically, socially and politically empowered through self-employment. Hence, the concept of women empowerment gained momentum in the recent decades. Microfinance, which evolved as a systematic financing approach in recent times through the network of co-operatives, commercial banks, regional rural banks, NABARD and NGOs has been largely a supply driver. The present seminar intends to focus light on different dimensions of microfinance and women empowerment through discussions and deliberations made by the eminent speakers, government regulators, corporate executives, researchers, academia, and practical experiences shared by the SHG members on various dimensions like Government Schemes, financial institutions, and microfinance and economic development its challenges and opportunities in particular and women empowerment in general.

Editor

Acknowledgements

This seminar volume has emerged with the contributions of a number of people. I take this opportunity to express my deep gratitude to all those, whose support made it possible for this national seminar volume to surface.

I would like to express my deepest thanks to the Advisory Committee Prof. Arjula Ramachandra Reddy, Hon'ble Vice Chancellor; Prof. C. Sivarami Reddy, Registrar and BOS Chairman; Prof M. Ramakrishna Reddy, Principal; Prof. K. Vali Pasha, Dean, School of Management Studies, Yogi Vemana University, Kadapa, for their constant encouragement and moral support in organizing the seminar.

I am particularly indebted to my faculty Prof. C. Sivarami Reddy and Prof. P. Mohan Reddy whose unstinted support helped me to design this seminar and to bring out this book.

I am grateful to all the invited speakers, guests of honour, paper contributors for their timely contribution to make this seminar as a fruitful to the others.

I am thankful to my colleagues Dr. Y. Subbarayudu, Saritha, Harinatha Reddy, Rajani, Abraham and students of M.Com for their care and cooperation at all stages of this work and bringing out this volume.

I would like to thank the publisher, Discovery Publishing House Pvt. Ltd. in bringing out this book. Last but not least a word of gratitude to my family members and to the Almighty, whose benevolence I ever beseech.

G. VIJAYA BHARATHI

Contents

Introduction

Microfinance

Microfinance is the provision of financial services to low income clients or solidarity lending groups including consumers and the self-employed, who traditionally lack access to banking and related services. More broadly, it is a movement whose object is "a world in which as many poor and near poor households as possible have permanent access to an appropriate range of high quality financial services, including not just credit but also savings, insurance, and fund transfers." Those who 'promote microfinance generally believe that such access will help poor people out of poverty. Microfinance, as is being practised could be defined as a set of services comprising the following activities.

Micro-Credit

Small loans are primarily for income generation activities, but also for consumption and contingency needs.

Micro-Savings

Thrift or small savings from borrowers' own resources.

Main features

The main features of the microfinance services being provided by MFIs are:

It is a tool for empowerment of the poorest; the higher the income and better the asset position of the borrower, the lower the incremental benefit from further equal doses of micro-credit is likely to be.

Delivery is normally through self-help groups.

It is essentially for promoting self-employment; the opportunities of wage employment are limited in developing countries—microfinance increases the productivity of self-employment in the informal sector of the economy—generally used for

- direct income generation
- rearrangement of assets and liabilities for the household to participate in future opportunities and
- consumption smoothing.

It is not just a financing system, but a tool for social change, specially for women—it does not spring from market forces alone—it is potentially welfare enhancing—there is a public interest in promoting the growth of microfinance—this is what makes it acceptable as a valid goal for public policy. Because micro-credit is aimed at the poorest, microfinance lending technology needs to mimic the informal lenders rather than the formal sector lending. It has to:

- provide for seasonality
- allow repayment flexibility
- eschew bureaucratic and legal formalities
- fix a ceiling on loan sizes.

Purpose of microfinance

Microfinance is to improve the lives of poor and marginalized populations by granting them access to financial services. Most notoriously, this will mean giving access to credit, i.e., the possibility to borrow small sums at reasonable interest rates, often without collateral, to allow the self-employed market vendor, seamstress, taxi driver, farmer, etc., to 'invest in their activity, increase their income and thereby improve their family's standard of living. As these small businesses grow, they often offer employment to other members of the community. Other services by microfinance institutions include micro-insurances, which provide a financial cushion in case of sickness, death or disaster. Savings accounts are also extremely important, providing a secure place for clients to save money to cover emergencies, to build better homes or to educate their children. Many MFIs also propose non-financial services, such as health care, children, business development training, legal support, etc., or facilitate contacts with organizations in the community that offer such services. Microfinance services empower clients, increasing their self-esteem and independence. The positive effects of microfinance investments can be observed through a multitude of individual success stories.

Empowerment of women

Empowerment can give power to women to have control over the circumstances of their lives. Empowerment of women is critical not only for their own welfare but also for the development of the country. Empowerment in the context of women's development is a way of defining, challenging and overcoming barriers in a woman's life through which she increases her ability to shape her life and environment. It is an active, multi-dimensional process, which should enable women to realize their full identity and power in all spheres of life. India envisions a future in which Indian women are independent and self-reliant. It is unfortunate that because of centuries of inertia, ignorance and conservatism, the actual and potential role of women in the society has been ignored, preventing them from making their rightful contribution to social progress. It is also because of distorted and/or partial information about their contribution to family and society that they are denied their rightful status and access to developmental resources and services contributing to their marginalization. Studies have shown that rural women help in producing up to 80 per cent of food in developing countries, yet they are entitled to only a fraction of farm land, and access to just 10 per cent of credit and five per cent of extension advice.

Women must be empowered by enhancing their awareness, knowledge; skills and technology use of efficiency, thereby, facilitating overall development of the society. The concept of self-help groups (SHGs) is providing to be a helpful instrument for the women empowerment. SHG is an organization of rural poor, particularly of women that deliver micro-credit to undertake the entrepreneurial activity. Entrepreneurship development and income generating activities are a feasible solution for empowering women. It generates income and also provides flexible working hours according to the needs of homemakers. Participation in income-generating activities helps in the overall empowerment of women.

Role of women in society

A woman has diversified functions to perform in the family as user, conserver, protector and creator/promoter of resources. Only thing is, they do not use, the modern jargons coined by the experts. Gone are the days when a man could boast of being capable of feeding the whole family. Now the woman must supplement it through whatever skill she has acquired. Now the women are playing multi-disciplinary roles. Such as

- Community organizer
- Family and Kinship Maintainer
- Mother
- Sister
- Wife
- Housekeeper
- Income Earner

In the process of conceptualizing the term entrepreneur, it is noted that though it is originated in the west, it has undergone many changes from time to time. Woman entrepreneur is an individual who takes up a challenging role in which she constantly interacts and adjusts herself with social, resource and support spheres in a society. By enabling women to become entrepreneurs and to participate fully and more effectively in a wide range of economic and especially industrial activities, they improve their position and also make greater progress towards higher economic growth, improved productivity, improved distribution of income, reduction in poverty and unemployment. The quality of women entrepreneurship is essentially influenced by the family and its immediate environment. The culture in which they are born and reared makes them depend on family members, friends and neighbors for decision-making in issues related to day to day living. The family support influences the entrepreneurial success of women.

1

Women Empowerment through SHGs

An Evidence from Bangalore Rural District, Karnataka

***G. Sudharshan Reddy**
****Dr. C. Sivarami Reddy**
*****Prof. P. Mohan Reddy**

ABSTRACT

Microfinance programs like the Self Help Bank Linkage Program in India have been increasingly promoted for their positive economic impact and the belief that they empower women. The present paper is an attempt to analyze the impact of self-help groups on women empowerment in Bangalore Rural District, Karnataka. The study uses various indicators like women's household decision-making power, financial autonomy, freedom of movement, political participation, acceptance of unequal gender role, exposure to media, access to education, and experience of domestic violence. The data required for the study collected through the distribution of structured questionnaire to 300 SHGs women members. The study reveals that women members of SHGs are empowered but the level of empowerment is less. They have taken control over their loans and they are

* Dept. of MBA, Acharya Institute of Management & Sciences, Bangalore-560058

** Professor, Department of Commerce, Sri Venkateswara University, Tirupati-517 502, A.P.

*** Associate Professor, Department of Commerce, Sri Venkateswara University, Tirupati-517 502, A.P.

able to manage them; participated in purchase decisions in the group and pricing of final products in the SHG and also at home; their self-confidence and mobility have improved; understand the importance of nutrition in the household, taking better care of health and hygiene of their family; they feel that their financial problems at home have come down; they are aware of the local government official, a Member of Legislative Assembly, a Member of Parliament, and the Prime Minister; and they are also aware of the legal procedures—like a man beating his wife, a man divorcing or abandoning his wife, unfair wages, unfair prices, high-handedness of police or government officials. The study concludes that SHGs women members in Bangalore Rural District, Karnataka, have empowered.

*(**Keywords:** Microfinance, Self-Help Groups, Women Empowerment.)*

Introduction

"At first, my family members did not count me worthy to be called when there was a problem or decision-making, but now through SHG I am given opportunity to participate in decision making" —**Lakshmi**,

A SHG member in Bangalore Rural District

The empowerment of women is one of the central issues in the process of development of countries all over the world. The empowerment of rural women is crucial for the development of the Rural Bharat. Bringing women into the mainstream of development is a major concern for the Government of India, which is why 2001 has been declared as the "Year of Women Empowerment". The programmes for Poverty Alleviation have a women's component to ensure flow of adequate funds to this section.

Pioneering microfinance institutions (MFIs) have already recognized that the twin goals of empowering women and developing poor communities are closely connected. The Nobel Prize-winning Grameen Bank, for example, gives around 96 per cent of its micro-loans to women, while the UN estimates that around 76 per cent of all microfinance clients globally are women. There are two different ways to look at this: one is that microfinance is good for women; the other is that women are good for microfinance, says Susy Cheston of Opportunity International, a US-based organization that gives around 86 per cent of its micro-credit loans to women. There are lots of different reasons that people lend to women. For some, it's about having customers that are very credit-worthy and bring better value to the institution.[1]

Before we understand the concept of women empowerment it is better to have some understanding about Indian public policy for rural finance and evolution of microfinance in India.

Evolution of microfinance in India

Indian public policy for rural finance from 1950s to till date mirrors the patterns observed worldwide. Increasing access to credit for the poor has always remained at the core of Indian planning in fight against poverty. The assumption behind expanding outreach of financial services, mainly credit was that the welfare costs of exclusion from the banking sector, especially for rural poor are very high. Starting late 1960s, India was home to one of largest state intervention in rural credit market and has been euphemistically referred to as 'Social banking' phase. This trend has been the product of a long evolution of the financial sector, which can be characterized by three major events.

Nationalisation of commercial banks

The first of these pivotal events was Indira Gandhi's bank nationalization drive launched in 1969, which required commercial banks to open rural branches resulting in a 15.2 per cent increase in rural bank branches in India between 1973 and 1985. Today, India has over 32,000 rural branches of commercial banks and regional rural banks, 14,000 cooperative bank branches, 98,000 primary agricultural credit societies (PACs), and 154,000 postal outlets that are required to focus on deposit mobilization and money transfers. India's deep financial system is attributable to its vast network of financial institutions. Unfortunately, the World Bank indicates that following bank nationalization, the share of banks in rural household debt increased to approximately 61.2 per cent in 1991.[2] Despite these achievements, there still has been little progress in providing the rural poor with access to formal finance. Rural banks serve primarily the needs of richer rural borrowers with some 66 per cent of large farmers having a deposit account and 44 per cent with access to credit in contrast to 70 per cent of marginal/landless farmers that do not have a bank account and 87 per cent that are without access to credit. Access to other financial services such as insurance are even more limited for the rural poor.[3]

Introduction of Integrated Rural Development Program (IRDP)

The second national policy that has had a significant impact on the evolution of India's banking and financial system is the Integrated Rural Development Program (IRDP) introduced in 1978 and designed to be 'a direct instrument for attacking India's rural poverty.' This program is interesting in this paper is because it was a large program whose main thrust was to alleviate poverty through the provision of loans and it was considered a failure. It therefore provides a comparison of what has failed in the past and how this affects the provision of microfinance through private means today. The IRDP was reputed as one of the largest poverty alleviation programs in the world with the number of loans advanced since its inception having reached approximately 45 million Indians with financial assistance worth US $6.17 billion disbursed.[4] Despite the massive support for the IRDP however, a government evaluation in 1989 revealed that it had not achieved the expected results with only 28 per cent of those assisted under the IRDP crossing the poverty line in contrast to private sector-led services and business micro-enterprises which performed better with 33 per cent of those involved in the sector that crossed the poverty line. The means through which the IRDP endeavored to provide the poor with access to productive assets was credit advanced by commercial banks, which the government subsidized. The subsidy provided by the government varied from 25 per cent for small farmers to 50 per cent for scheduled castes and tribal people. The overarching goal of the program was to enhance the income of the rural poor sufficiently so as to enable them to cross the poverty line.[5] Therefore, by this standard the IRDP did not achieve its expected results.

Liberalization of India's financial system

The last major event which impacted the financial and banking system in India was the liberalization of India's financial system in the 1990s characterized by a series of structural adjustments and financial policy reforms initiated by the Reserve Bank of India (RBI). The result was a partial deregulation of interest rates, increased competition in the banking sector, and new microfinance approaches of which the most notable was a movement to link informal local groups called self-help groups (SHGs) created by NGOs to commercial banks like the National Bank for Agriculture and Rural Development (NABARD). These financial policy reforms in the 1990s were very significant to microfinance because they involved scrapping the interest rate controls for credit to the poor and other types of credit. These financial liberalization measures then made it possible for NABARD to transform what was then a small research project into a full-blown microfinance program for the whole country.

This program was better known as the 'SHG Bank Linkage' model, which has come to be one of the most well-known and widespread microfinance models in India.[6] Since many consider the SHG Bank Linkage model of microfinance to be one of the major successes of microfinance delivery in the country it will provide the most important direct contrast to the delivery of microfinance services by individual MFIs. The number of women's SHGs linked to banks was reported at 800,000 in 2004 by the World Bank. The rough estimate of women reached was about 12 million. Originally, NABARD provided subsidized refinancing to encourage banks to lend to SHGs, although the demand declined as banks began to discover that SHG lending is quite profitable. Banks would lend to SHGs at about 12 per cent per annum and groups would on-lend to individual members at a rate they determine, typically this would be around 24 per cent per annum.[7] The hypothesis for why individual MFIs not reached as many poor as the SHG Bank Linkage program has been that individual MFIs have been constrained mainly due to lack of resources and capital. Another important point to consider is that the SHG Bank Linkage model is dependent on the formation of SHGs, something that in India has been done by NGOs and therefore requires subsidy. This provides a helpful separation of activities that require subsidy, the creation of SHGs, and those that can operate on a commercial basis such as bank lending to those SHGs.

Empowerment of women—Concept

Empowerment is a multi-faceted, multi-dimensional and multi-layered concept. Most of us, when asked, have a great deal of difficulty defining empowerment. The word does not even translate literally into many languages. Yet most of us know empowerment when we see it. There are several interpretations about empowerment of women. The following are the few important ones:

Krishna defines empowerment as "the process of increasing the capacity of individuals or groups to make choices and to transform those choices into desired actions and outcomes. Central to this process are actions that both build individual and collective assets, and improve the efficiency and fairness of the organizational and institutional context which govern the use of these assets."[8] Kabeer stresses, "women's empowerment is about the process by which those who have been denied the ability to make strategic life choices acquire such ability."[9] According to her it is important to understand empowerment as a process and not an instrumentalist form of advocacy, which requires measurement and quantification of empowerment. Kabeer emphasizes that the ability to exercise choice incorporates three interrelated dimensions: resources, agency and achievements.

Resources

Resources can be material, social or human. In other words, they refer not only to conventional economic resources, such as land, equipment, finance, working capital etc. but also to the various human and social resources, which serve to enhance the ability to exercise choice. Human resources are embodied in the individual and encompass his or her knowledge, skills, creativity, imagination and so on. Social resources, on the other hand, are made up of the claims, obligations and expectations which inhere in the relationships, networks and connections which prevail in different spheres of life and which enable people to improve their situation and life chances beyond what would be possible through their individual efforts alone.

Resources are distributed through a variety of different institutions and processes and access to resources will be determined by the rules, norms and practices, which prevail in different institutional domains (e.g. familial norms, patron-client relationships, informal wage agreements, formal contractual transactions, and public sector entitlements). These rules, norms and practices give some actors authority over others in determining the principles of distribution and exchange within that sphere. Consequently, the distribution of 'allocative' resources tends to be embedded within the distribution of 'authoritative resources', the ability to define priorities and enforce claims. Heads of households, chiefs of tribes, directors of firms, managers of organisations, elites within a community are all endowed with decision-making authority within particular institutional contexts by virtue of their positioning within those institutions.

The terms on which people gain access to resources are as important as the resources themselves when the issue of empowerment is being considered. Access may be conditional on highly clientilist forms of dependency relationships or extremely exploitative conditions of work or it may be achieved in ways, which offer dignity and a sense of self-worth. Empowerment entails a change in the terms on which resources are acquired as much as an increase in access to resources.

Agency

The second dimension of power relates to agency, the ability to define one's goals and act upon them. Agency is about more than observable action; it also encompasses the meaning, motivation and purpose, which individuals bring to their activity, their sense of agency, or 'the power within'. While agency often tends to be operationalised as 'individual decision making', particularly in the mainstream economic literature, in reality, it encompasses a much wider range of purposive actions, including bargaining, negotiation, deception, manipulation, subversion, resistance and protest as well as the more intangible, cognitive processes of reflection and analysis. Agency also encompasses collective, as well as individual, reflection and action.

Agency has both positive and negative meanings in relation to power. In the positive sense of the 'power to', it refers to people's capacity to define their own life-choices and to pursue their own goals, even in the face of opposition from others. Agency can also be exercised in the more negative sense of 'power over', in other words, the capacity of an actor or category of actors to over-ride the agency of others, for instance, through the use of violence, coercion and threat. However, power can also operate in the absence of any explicit agency. The norms and rules governing social behaviour tend to ensure that certain outcomes are reproduced without any apparent exercise of agency. Where these outcomes bear on the strategic life choices noted earlier, they testify to the exercise of power as 'non-decision-making' (Lukes). The norms of marriage in South Asia, for instance, invest parents with the authority for choosing their children's partners, but are unlikely to be experienced as a form of power—unless such authority is questioned.

Achievements

Resources and agency together constitute what Sen refers to as capabilities, the potential that people have for living the lives they want, of achieving valued ways of 'being and doing'. Sen uses the idea of 'functioning' to refer to all the possible ways of 'being and doing' which are valued by people in a given context and of 'functioning achievements' to refer to the particular ways of being and doing which are realised by different individuals. These realised achievements, or the failure to do so, constitute our third dimension of power. Clearly, where the failure to achieve valued ways of 'being and doing' can be traced to laziness, incompetence or some other reason particular to an individual, then the issue of power is not relevant. When, however, the failure to achieve reflects asymmetries in the underlying distribution of capabilities, it can be taken as a manifestation of disempowerment.

Thus one may conclude that by helping women meet their practical needs and increase their efficacy in their traditional roles, microfinance can help women to gain respect and achieve more in their traditional roles, which in turn can lead to increased esteem and self-confidence. Although increased esteem does not automatically lead to empowerment, it does contribute decisively to women's ability and willingness to challenge the social injustices and discriminatory systems that they face.

From the above we can say women's empowerment is a process in which women gain greater share of control over resources—material, human and intellectual like knowledge, information, ideas and financial resources like money—and access to money and control over decision-making in the home, community, society and nation, and to gain 'power'. Put in simple, "Empowerment means moving from a position of enforced powerlessness to one of power".

Empowerment frameworks used in microfinance

Schuler, Hashemi and Riley's Empowerment Index uses eight indicators, each including a variety of specific actions or items:[10]

1. *Freedom of mobility:* Mobility refers to going to the market, a medical facility, and the movies, outside the village.
2. *Ability to make small purchases:* Purchasing small items used daily in food preparation for the family (kerosine, cooking oil, and spices), small items for herself, (hair oil, soap, glass bangles), purchasing ice cream or sweets for children. And sometimes decisions were normally made without asking the husband's permission, and if the purchases were made at least in part with money earned by the respondent herself.
3. *Ability to make larger purchases:* Large purchases like pots and pans, children's clothing, saris for herself and buying the family's daily food. And sometimes the purchases were made at least in part with money earned by the respondent herself.
4. *Involvement in major household decisions:* Involvement in decision (individually or jointly with

the husband) within the past few years about house repair or renovation, deciding to lease land and buy land, a boat or a bicycle rickshaw.

5. *Relative freedom from domination by the family:* Here freedom to buy land, jewelry or livestock from her own money, or purchases made in the family against her will.
6. *Political and legal awareness:* Knowing the name of a local government official, a Member of Parliament, and the Prime Minister and the significance of registering a marriage and knowing the law governing inheritance like comes under political and legal awareness.
7. *Involvement in political campaigning and protests:* Just awareness sometimes may not be empowered, but they should involve in campaigning for political candidate or had gotten together with others to protest: a man beating his wife, a man divorcing or abandoning his wife, unfair wages, unfair prices. Misappropriation of relief goods. Or high-handedness of police or government officials.
8. *Economic security and contribution to family support:* Economic security have when woman owned her house or homestead land, owning any productive asset, having her own cash savings and savings were ever used for business or money-lending.

Basic views of the link between microfinance and women's empowerment

There are four basic views on the link between microfinance and women's empowerment:[11]

1. There are those who stress the positive evidence and are essentially optimistic about the possibility of sustainable microfinance programmes world-wide empowering women;

2. Another school of thought recognizes the limitations to empowerment, but explains those with poor programme design;
3. Others recognize the limitations of microfinance for promoting empowerment, but see it as a key ingredient as important in themselves within a strategy to alleviate poverty; empowerment in this view needs to be addressed by other means;
4. Then there are those who see microfinance programmes as a waste of resources.

In the present study we study and support the view of Microfinance and women empowerment.

Objectives of the study

The prime objective of the study is to know the impact of SHGs on Women Empowerment with special reference to SHGs operating in Thyamagondlu village, Bangalore Rural District, Karnataka. The secondary objectives of the study are:

1. To trace the evolution of microfinance in India,
2. To understand the concept of women empowerment,
3. Empowerment frameworks used in microfinance,
4. Basic views of the link between microfinance and women's empowerment,
5. To know the impact of SHGs on women empowerment.

Methodology of the study

The study is descriptive in nature. The population of the study consists of all the members (around 900) of the Self-Help Groups operating in Thyamagondlu village, Bangalore Rural District, Karnataka. With the use of convenience sampling method the researcher has selected 300 SHG women members as sample size for the study. See Table 1.1 for detailed sample size from each area.

The data have been collected from primary as well as secondary sources. The primary data have been obtained from respondents through distribution of questionnaire. The secondary data have been collected from Internet, magazine, editorials, government rules and regulations on finance and microfinance.

Note: All the tables presented in the study are constructed based on the primary data.

Table 1.1: Distribution of sample size on the basis of area

Self-Help Group	Village	Sample Size
Mahimashree Mahila Swasahaya Sangha	Kannuhalli	20
Stree Shakthi Sangha	Manne	20
Imdiragandhi Swa Sahaya Sangha	Thyamagondlu	120
Jannath Muslim Mahila Swa Sahaya Sangha	Thyamagondlu	20
Rani Chennamma Mahila Swa Sahaya Sangha	Thvarekere	20
Sonia Gandhi Mahila Swa Sahaya Sangha	Muddalinganahalli	20
Stree Shakthi Sangha	Rampur	20
Jai Bharat Stree Shakthi Sangha	Obalapur	20
Sri Ganesh Stree Sangha	Vinayakanagar	20
Stree Shakthi Sangha	Kuntabhommanahalli	20
Total		**300**

Demographic characteristics

Demography refers to the characteristics of the population. Demographics are the vital statistics that describe population. People constitute markets; demographics are of special interest to marketing executives. Demographic characteristics include gender, age, education, occupation, monthly family income, and family size for marketing their products. In the present study gender, age and education has been covered. Table 1.2 depicts the demographic characteristic of respondents

Age

Table 1.2 indicates that 50 per cent of the respondents are falling in the age group of 36-45. At the same time members age ranges between 16 years to 65 years. It indicates that age is not the basis for SHG membership; any person who is unemployed can join in the SHG.

Education

From Table 1.2 it is clear that 92 per cent of the respondents are falling in the education level that is SSLC and less than SSLC. It shows that members do not have jobs due to low education qualification. SHG membership is for unemployed and it is not based on the education qualification.

Table 1.2: Demographic characteristics of respondents

Characteristics	No. of Respondents	Percentage
Age		
< 15	00	00
16- 25	06	02
26- 35	30	10
36-45	150	50
46-55	90	30
56- 65	24	8
> 65	00	00
Education		
< SSLC	240	80
SSLC	36	12
PUC	24	8
> Degree	00	00

As said in Table 1.2 SHG membership is for unemployed and it is not for a specific age group, education level and not on the basis of specific cast (see Table 1.3).

Table 1.3: Caste-wise distributions of respondents

Caste	No. of Respondents	Percentage
Brahmin	60	20
Vokkaliga	42	14
Lingayat	48	16
SC	36	12
ST	42	14
Others	72	24
Total	**300**	**100**

Impact of SHGs on women empowerment

Table 1.4 shows that 80 per cent SHGs members (women) have taken control over their loans and they are able to manage them. Another concern is over the feminization of debt, where women are seen as becoming mediators between the male members of their family and the microfinance institutions. We can say that it is an indication of women empowerment.

Table 1.4: Control of their loans and management

Opinion	No. of Respondents	Percentage
Yes	240	80
No	60	20
Total	**300**	**100**

Table 1.5: Participation in purchasing decisions at home and in the SHG

Opinion	No. of Respondents	Percentage
Yes	231	77
No	69	23
Total	**300**	**100**

Generally rural women do not participate in purchasing decision. But, as evident from Table 1.5, women (77%) after joining SHGs are able to participate in purchase decisions at home. Not only they participate in decision-making at home they also participated in purchase of raw materials and pricing of final products in the SHG.

Table 1.6: Increased self-confidence and mobility

Opinion	No. of Respondents	Percentage
Yes	264	88
No	36	12
Total	**300**	**100**

The level of self-confidence and mobility are also important constituents of empowerment. It is very interesting to see that 88 per cent (Table 1.6) of the respondents opinion that their confidence level and mobility has increased after joining the group. This helped members in expressing their opinions in meetings. The interaction with officials had greatly increased and was an indicator of greater mobility, confidence, exposure and better communication skills.

Table 1.7: Decision-making within the household

Opinion	No. of Respondents	Percentage
Family Planning	237	79
Children's Marriage	252	84
Buying and Selling Assets	135	45
Sending Daughter to School	225	74

From Table 1.7 we can say that SHG members (above 75% of women) have involvement in the decision-making in their family planning, children's marriage, buying and selling assets, sending daughter to school. These decisions, which have traditionally been within the male domain, reflect that although the women have been empowered, SHGs have not been able to positively impact their decision-making in buying and selling assets. A slight change, however, has been noticed in the inclusion of women in the decision-making process of sending their daughters to school.

Table 1.8: Improving efficiency of activities that are culturally considered within the woman's domain.

Opinion	No. of Respondents	Percentage
Improved nutrition in the household	207	69
Taking better care of health and hygiene of their children	219	73
Helping in social functions, such as weddings	240	80

Table 1.8 indicates that SHG women members improved their efficiency in nutrition in the household (69%), taking better care of health and hygiene of their children (73%); and helping in the social functions like marriage and even started celebrating children's birth days.

Table 1.9: Reduction of tough times in SHG members' families after joining SHGs

Opinion	No. of Respondents	Percentage
Decreased	195	65
No Impact	105	35
Total	**300**	**100**

Table 1.9 shows that 65 per cent of the respondents feel that financial problems at home came down due to joining SHGs and start working in the groups. But there are 35 per cent of the people directly say that there is no impact of SHGs on their families.

Table 1.10: Political and legal awareness among SHG members

Opinion	No. of Respondents	Percentage
Aware	225	75
Not aware	75	25
Total	**300**	**100**

Awareness about political and legal procedures increased among SHG women members (75%). They are aware of the local government official, a Member of Legislative Assembly, a Member of Parliament, and the Prime Minister. They are also aware of the legal procedures—like a man beating his wife, a man divorcing or abandoning his wife, unfair wages, unfair prices, high-handedness of police or government officials.

Findings from the study

From the foregoing analysis and interpretation the following findings have been extracted:

- Half of the respondents are falling in the age group of 36-45. At the same time members age ranges between 16 years to 65 years. It indicates that age is not the basis for SHG membership; any person who is unemployed can join the SHG.
- About 92 per cent of the respondents are falling in the education level that is SSLC and less than SSLC and they do not have jobs due to low education qualification. It indicates that SHG membership is for unemployed and it is not based on the education qualification, any body can join the SHG. At the same time there is no discrimination among different cast people; SHG membership is opened for all the casts. In other words, it is not for a specific age group, education level and not on the basis of specific cast
- Majority of the SHG members have taken control

over their loans and they are able to manage them. Another concern is over the feminization of debt, where women are seen as becoming mediators between the male members of their family and the microfinance institutions.

- Generally rural women do not participate in purchasing decision. But the present study shows that 77 per cent of the SHG members were able to participate in purchase decisions and pricing of final products. They also participate in decision-making at home.
- Self-confidence and mobility are also important constituents of empowerment. It is very interesting to see that 88 per cent of the respondents feel that their confidence level and mobility has increased after joining the group. These helped members in expressing their opinions in meetings, in interaction with officials and were an indicator of greater mobility, confidence, exposure and better communication skills.
- Above 75 per cent of SHG members have involved in decision-making in their family like family planning, children's marriage, buying and selling assets, sending daughter to school. These decisions, which have traditionally been within the male domain, reflect that the women have been empowered. But SHGs have not been able to positively impact their decision-making in buying and selling assets. A slight change, however, has been noticed in the inclusion of women in the decision-making process of sending their daughters to school.
- One very interesting thing to note here is that SHG members were able to understand the importance of nutrition in the household, taking better care of health and hygiene of their family. They also started in helping in the social functions like marriage and even started celebrating children's birthdays.

- Majority of the respondents feel that financial problems at home have come down due to joining SHGs and start working in the groups.
- Awareness about political and legal procedures increased among SHG women members. They are aware of the local government official, a Member of Legislative Assembly, a Member of Parliament, and the Prime Minister. They are also aware of the legal procedures—like a man beating his wife, a man divorcing or abandoning his wife, unfair wages, unfair prices, high-handedness of police or government officials.
- One very interesting thing to disclose here is that empowerment also led conflicts in some of the SHG members' family. The house owners disclosed this.

From the above findings we can definitely say that SHGs helped women empowerment.

Conclusion

The empowerment of women is one of the central issues in the process of development of countries all over the world and it is also crucial for the development of the Rural Bharat. Bringing women into the mainstream of development is a major concern for the Government of India. Pioneering microfinance institutions (MFIs) have already recognized that the twin goals of empowering women and developing poor communities are closely connected. The Nobel Prize-winning Grameen Bank, for example, gives around 96 per cent of its micro-loans to women, while the UN estimates that around 76 per cent of all microfinance clients globally are women. Indian public policy for rural finance from 1950s to till date mirrors the patterns observed worldwide. Increasing access to credit for the poor has always remained at the core of Indian planning in fight against poverty. Starting late 1960s, India was home to one of largest state intervention in rural credit market and has been euphemistically referred to as 'Social banking' phase. This trend has been the product of a long evolution of the financial sector, which can be characterized by three major events—nationalisation of commercial banks; introduction of integrated rural development program (IRDP) and liberalization of India's financial system. IRDP program was better known as the 'SHG Bank Linkage' model, which has come to be one of the most well-known and widespread microfinance models in India. Women empowerment is the process of increasing the capacity of individuals or groups to make choices and to transform those choices into desired actions and outcomes. As per Schuler, Hashemi and Riley's empowerment index most of the SHGs members in Thyamagondlu village, Bangalore Rural District, Karnataka, were empowered, but the level of empowerment need to be improved. At the same time there is a need to educate empowered women in reducing conflicts at home particularly with head of the house.

REFERENCES

1. Valdis Wish, *Microfinance: A Platform for the Empowerment of Women*, Allianz Knowledge Partnersite, January 6, 2006 (Accessed from *knowledge.allianz.com* on 6-2-2009).
2. Basu and Srivastava, *Scaling-up Microfinance for India's Rural Poor*, World Bank Policy Research Working Paper 3646, June 2005, p. 4. Accessed Jan. 2009. Available from: *http://www.worldbank.org*.
3. *Ibid.*, p. 5.
4. Remenyi and Quinones, *Microfinance and Poverty Alleviation: Case Studies from Asia and the Pacific* (Edited), New York: Pinter, 2000, p. 86.
5. *Ibid.*, p. 87.
6. *Ibid.*, p. 92.
7. Basu and Srivastava, *op.cit.*, p. 12.
8. Krishna A, *Social Capital, Community Driven Development, and Empowerment: A short note on concepts and operations*, World Bank Working Paper 33077, 2003, WB, Washington, DC.

9. *Microfinance and Women's Empowerment—Evidence from the Self Help Group Bank Linkage Programme in India*, SIDA (A Division for Market Development), September, 2006, p. 9.
10. Linda Mayoux, 2005, *Gender Equity, Equality and Women's Empowerment: Principles, Definitions and Frameworks*, p. 9. (Accessed from Aga Khan Foundation website on *Microfinance for Women's Empowerment*, on Feb 2009).
11. Linda Mayoux, *Microfinance and the Empowerment of Women—A Review of the Key Issues*, p. 3.

2

Women Empowerment through Microfinance

Challenges and Opportunities

*G. Venkatachalam
**Dr. P. Mohan Reddy

ABSTRACT

In India, the trickle down effects of macroeconomic policies have failed to resolve the problem of gender inequality. Women have been the vulnerable section of society and constitute a sizeable segment of the poverty-struck population. Women face gender specific barriers to access education health, employment etc. Microfinance deals with women below the poverty line. Micro-loans are available solely and entirely to this target group of women. There are several reasons for this: among the poor, the poor women are most disadvantaged, they are characterized by lack of education and access to resources, both of which is required to help them work their way out of poverty and for upward economic and social mobility. The problem is more acute for women in countries like India, despite the fact that women's labour makes a critical contribution to the economy. This is due to the low social status and lack of access to key resources. Evidence shows that groups of women are better customers than men, the better

* Ph.D., Research Scholar, Department of Commerce, Sri Venkateswara University, Tirupati-517 502, A.P.

** Associate Professor, Department of Commerce, Sri Venkateswara University, Tirupati-517 502, A.P.

managers of resources. If loans are routed through women benefits of loans are spread wider among the household.

The present paper seeks to identify the challenges of Microfinance with respect to poverty alleviation and socio-economic empowerment of rural women. An effort is also made to suggest the ways to enhance women empowerment. India is the country where a collaborative model between banks, NGOs, MFIs and women's organizations is furthest advanced. It, therefore, serves as a good starting point to look at what we know so far about 'Best Practice' in relation to microfinance for women's empowerment and how different institutions can work together. It is clear that gender strategies in microfinance need to look beyond just increasing women's access to savings and credit and organizing self-help groups to look strategically at how programmes can actively promote gender equality and women's empowerment. Moreover the focus should be on developing a diversified microfinance sector where different type of organizations—NGO, MFIs and formal sector banks—all should have gender policies adapted to the needs of their particular target groups/institutional roles and capacities and collaborate and work together to make a significant contribution to gender equality and pro-poor development.

Introduction

In India, the trickle down effects of macroeconomic policies have failed to resolve the problem of gender inequality. Women have been the vulnerable section of society and constitute a sizeable segment of the poverty-struck population. Women face gender specific barriers to access education, health, employment etc. Microfinance deals with women below the poverty line. Micro-loans are available solely and entirely to this target group of women. There are several reasons for this: among the poor, the poor women are most disadvantaged, they are characterized by lack of education and access to resources, both of which is required to help them work their way out of poverty and for upward economic and social mobility.

The problem is more acute for women in countries like India, despite the fact that women's labour makes a critical contribution to the economy. This is due to the low social status and lack of access to key resources. Evidence shows that groups of women are better customers than men, the better managers of resources. If loans are routed through women, benefits of loans are spread wider among the household.

Aim of the paper

The present paper seeks to identify the challenges of Microfinance with respect to poverty alleviation and socio-economic empowerment of rural women. An effort is also made to suggest the ways to enhance women empowerment.

Women empowerment—The concept

Since women's empowerment is the key to socio-economic development of the community; bringing women into the mainstream of national development has been a major concern of government. The Ministry of Rural Development has special components for women in its programmes. Funds are earmarked as "Women's component" to ensure flow of adequate resources for the same. Besides Swarnajayanti Grameen Swarozgar Yojana (SGSY), Ministry of Rural Development is implementing other scheme having women's component. They are—Indira Awas Yojana (IAJ), National Social Assistance Programme (NSAP), Restructured Rural Sanitation Programme, Accelerated Rural Water Supply Programme (ARWSP) the (erstwhile) Integrated Rural Development Programme (IRDP), the (erstwhile) Development of Women and Children in Rural Areas (DWCRA) and the Jowahar Rozgar Yojana (JRY).

Microfinance—The definition

The term microfinance is of recent origin and is commonly used in addressing issues related to poverty alleviation, financial support to micro-entrepreneurs, gender development etc. There is, however, no statutory definition of microfinance. The taskforce on Supportitative Policy and Regulatory Framework for Microfinance has defined microfinance as "Provision of thrift, credit and other financial services and products of very small amounts to the poor in rural, semi-urban or urban areas for enabling them to raise their income levels and improve living standards". The term "Micro" literally means "small". But the taskforce has not defined any amount. However as per Micro Credit Special Cell of the Reserve Bank of India, the borrower amounts up to the limit of Rs. 25000 could be considered as micro-credit products and this amount could be gradually increased up to Rs. 40000 over a period of time which roughly equals to $500 – a standard for South Asia as per international perceptions.

The term microfinance, sometimes is used interchangeably with the term micro-credit. However while micro-credit refers to purveyance of loans in small quantities, the term microfinance has a broader meaning covering in its ambit other financial services like saving, insurance etc. as well. The mantra "Microfinance" is banking through groups. The essential features of the approach are to provide financial services through the groups of individuals, formed either in joint liability or co-obligation mode. The other dimensions of the microfinance approach are:

- Savings/thrift proceeds credit
- Credit is linked with savings/thrift
- Absence of subsidies
- Group plays an important role in credit appraisal, monitoring and recovery.

Types of SHGs

Self-Help Groups (SHGs)

The group in this case does financial intermediation on behalf of the formal institution. This is the predominant model followed in India.

Grameen groups

In this model, financial assistance is provided to the individual in a group by the formal institution on the strength of group's assurance. In other words, individual loans are provided on the strength of joint liability/co-obligation. This microfinance model was initiated by Bangladesh Grameen Bank and is being used by some of the Microfinance Institutions (MFIs) in India.

Concern with women's access to credit and assumptions about contributions to women's empowerment are not new. From the early 1970s women's movements in a number of countries became increasingly interested in the degree to which women were able to access poverty-focused credit programmes and credit cooperatives. In India organizations like Self-Employed Women's Association (SEWA) among others with origins and affiliations in the Indian labour and women's movements identified credit as a major constraint in their work with informal sector women workers.

MICROFINANCE INSTRUMENT AND NEW ECONOMY

Microfinance is emerging as a powerful instrument for poverty alleviation in the new economy. In India, microfinance scene is dominated by Self-Help Groups (SHGs)-Bank Linkage Programme, aimed at providing a cost-effective mechanism for providing financial services to the "unreached poor". Based on the philosophy of peer pressure and group savings as collateral substitute, the SHG programme has been successful in not only in meeting peculiar needs of the rural poor, but also in strengthening collective self-help capacities of the poor at the local level, leading to their empowerment.

Microfinance for the poor and women has received extensive recognition as a strategy for poverty reduction and for economic empowerment. Increasingly in the last five years, there is questioning of whether micro-credit is most effective approach to economic empowerment of poorest and, among them, women in particular. Development practitioners in India and developing countries often argue that the exaggerated focus on microfinance as a solution for the poor has led to neglect by the state and public institutions in addressing employment and livelihood needs of the poor.

Credit for empowerment is about organizing people, particularly around credit and building capacities to manage money. The focus is on getting the poor to mobilize their own funds, building their capacities and empowering them to leverage external credit. Perception of women is that learning to manage money and rotate funds builds women's capacities and confidence to intervene in local governance beyond the limited goals of ensuring access to credit. Further, it combines the goals of financial sustainability with that of creating community owned institutions.

Before 1990s, credit schemes for rural women were almost negligible. The concept of women's credit was born on the insistence by women-oriented studies that highlighted the discrimination and struggle of women in having the access of credit. However, there is a perceptible gap in financing genuine credit needs of the poor especially women in the rural sector. There are certain misconception about the poor people that they need loan at subsidized rate of interest on soft terms, they lack education, skill, capacity to save, credit worthiness and therefore are not bankable. Nevertheless, the experience of several SHGs reveal that rural poor are actually efficient managers of credit and finance. Availability of timely and adequate credit is essential for them to undertake any economic activity rather than credit subsidy.

The Government measures have attempted to help the poor by implementing different poverty alleviation programmes but with little success. Since most of them are target-based involving lengthy procedures for loan disbursement, high transaction costs, and lack of supervision and monitoring. Since the credit requirements of the rural poor cannot be adopted on project lending approach as it is in the case of organized sector, there emerged the need for an informal credit supply through SHGs. The rural poor with the assistance from NGOs have demonstrated their potential for self help to secure economic and financial strength. Various case studies show that there is a positive correlation between credit availability and women's empowerment.

Challenges of microfinance

Surveys have shown that many elements contribute to make it more difficult for women empowerment through micro-businesses. These elements are:

- Lack of knowledge of the market and potential profitability, thus making the choice of business difficult.
- Inadequate book-keeping.
- Employment of too many relatives which increases social pressure to share benefits.
- Setting prices arbitrarily.
- Lack of capital.
- High interest rates.
- Inventory and inflation accounting is never undertaken.
- Credit policies that can gradually ruin their business (many customers cannot pay cash; on the other hand, suppliers are very harsh towards women).

Other shortcomings

Burden of meeting

Time consuming meetings, in particular in programmes based on group lending, and time consuming income generating activities without reduction of traditional responsibilities increase women's work and time burden.

New pressures

By using social capital, in-group lending/group collateral programmes, additional stresses and pressures are introduced, which might increase vulnerability and reflect disempowerment.

Reinforcement of traditional gender roles:
Lack of economic empowerment

Microfinance assists women to perform traditional roles better and women thus remain trapped in low productivity sectors, not moving from the group of survival enterprises to micro-enterprises. There are evidence of men withdrawing their contributions to certain types of household expenditures.

Conclusion

A conclusion that emerges from this account is that microfinance can contribute to solving the problems of inadequate housing and urban services as an integral part of poverty alleviation programmes. The challenge lies in finding the level of flexibility in the credit instrument that could make it match the multiple credit requirements of the low income borrower without imposing unbearably high cost of monitoring its end use upon the lenders. A promising solution is to provide multi-purpose lone or composite credit for income generation, housing improvement and consumption support. Consumption loan is found to be especially important during the gestation period between commencing a new economic activity and deriving positive income. Careful research on demand for financing and savings behavior of the potential borrowers and their participation in determining the mix of multi-purpose loans are essential in making the concept work. The organizations involved in micro-credit initiatives should take account of the fact that:

- Credit is important for development but cannot by itself enable very poor women to overcome their poverty.
- Making credit available to women does not automatically mean they have control over its use and over any income they might generate from micro-enterprises.

- In situations of chronic poverty it is more important to provide saving services than to offer credit.
- A useful indicator of the tangible impact of micro-credit schemes is the number of additional proposals and demands presented by local villagers to public authorities.

Nevertheless ensuring that the microfinance sector continues to move forward in relation to gender equality and women's empowerment will require a long-term strategic process of the same order as the one in relation to poverty if gender is not to continue to 'evaporate' in a combination of complacency and resistance within donor agencies and the microfinance sector. This will involve:

- Ongoing exchange of experience and innovation between practitioners.
- Constant awareness and questioning of 'bad practice'.
- Lobbying donors for sufficient funding for empowerment strategies.
- Bringing together the different players in the sector to develop coherent policies and for gender advocacy.

India is the country where a collaborative model between banks, NGOs, MFIs and Women's organizations is furthest advanced. It therefore serves as a good starting point to look at what we know so far about 'Best Practice' in relation to microfinance for women's empowerment and how different institutions can work together. It is clear that gender strategies in microfinance need to look beyond just increasing women's access to savings and credit and organizing self-help groups to look strategically at how programmes can actively promote gender equality and women's empowerment. Moreover the focus should be on developing a diversified microfinance sector where different type of organizations—NGO, MFIs and formal sector banks—all should have gender policies adapted to the needs of their particular target groups/ institutional roles and capacities and collaborate and work together to make a significant contribution to gender equality and pro-poor development.

REFERENCES

1. Harper, Malcolm, 2002, "Promotion of Self Help Groups under the SHG Bank Linkage Program in India", Paper presented at the Seminar on SHG-bank Linkage Programme at New Delhi, November 25-26, 2002.
2. Kabeer, N., 2001, "Conflicts Over Credit: Re-evaluation the Empowerment Potential of Loans to Women in Rural Bangladesh": *World Development*, Vol. 29, No. 1.
3. Fisher, Thomas and M.S. Sriram ed., 2002, *Beyond Micro-credit: Putting Development Back into Microfinance*.

3

Microfinance and Women Empowerment

Problems and Prospects

*Prof. Chowdari Prasad
**Vamshi Krishna Arumbaka

ABSTRACT

Women have consistently contributed to the economic development of India for centuries. The average Indian woman plays many roles in life and contributes to the well-being of her family. Despite several claims and announcement of policies about their emancipation, very few women stand empowered. In most cases, lack of financial help is the bane. These loans are not huge but are micro-level which would help set up small cottage units like papad making, agarbatti manufacturing, daily trading of fruits and vegetables, etc. Many banks and financial institutions have been helping in this area but the gap is too big to be filled. Here comes the role of SHGs and NGOs.

Government Schemes and availability of institutional finance support microfinance initiatives fully. Some NGOs have done wonders when it comes to return on investment and the contribution to uplift the economic status of women. The paper looks at the success stories of leading women who have started

* Professor of Finance and Registrar, Alliance Business School, Bangalore-560 068, Email: chowdri.p@absindia.org

** PGP Student (Marketing), Alliance Business School, Bangalore-560 068, Email: vamshiavk@yahoo.com

at small level but built empires which in turn empower other women in the society by providing livelihood. The paper also looks at the problems encountered in the path and what are the prospects. Lijjat Papad, SEWA, AWAKE, FIWE,COWE and many more SHGs are shining examples of testimony for the change microfinance initiatives can bring in to empower the women.

Introduction

According to the Micro-credit Summit Campaign 2001 report, 14.2 million of the world's poorest women now have access to financial services through specialized microfinance institutions (MFIs), banks, NGOs, and other non-banking financial institutions. These women account for nearly 74 per cent of the 19.3 million of the world's poorest people now being served by microfinance institutions. Most of these women have access to credit to invest in businesses that they own and operate themselves. Majority of them have excellent repayment records, in spite of the daily hardships they face. Contrary to conventional wisdom, they have shown that it is a very noble idea to lend to the poor and to women. So, given these impressive statistics, can we pat ourselves on the back for our service to poor women and assume that women's empowerment and other gender issues will take care of themselves?

The way women empowerment is defined determines what should be prioritized and how it can be achieved. Women empowerment is a broad term to limit to a few things like employment, literacy, etc. It includes increasing the social status of women by providing better food, education, ownership of assets; eradicating poverty, and providing equal rights in a short time. Self-employment schemes and Microfinance taken up by government and NGOs have given commendable results in several countries like China, Korea, Italy, Australia, Africa, Indonesia and in India in states—Andhra Pradesh, Karnataka and Assam, and many other places. Microfinance is referred as the key to success of many self-help groups, entrepreneurial and self-managed ventures. But these ventures sometimes have a short lifespan and encounter several problems in the competitive world. This can be sustained by ensuring that micro-financial initiatives would have the desired results and implemented as per plan. Mere providing of money does not end the troubles of women nor do they empower them. Empowering is a long drawn process but has a fruitful end. How does microfinance achieve these initiatives is the key.

Microfinance: Prospects and problems

In the 1990s, microfinance captured the imagination of several opinion leaders, governments and donor agencies. Supporters of MF argue that microfinance institutions (MFIs) can not only have a major impact in the fight against poverty, but can do so on a sustainable basis to empower the beneficiaries. At the same time, a number of critics have also emerged. On the other hand, while it has been generally accepted that women managed MFIs can and should become financially self-sufficient, only few have actually done so. It may be appropriate for well-managed programs to receive some ongoing level of subsidization if they can be shown to be effective in reducing poverty. It is important that the focus should be on quality rather than quantity.

Microfinance is the provision of financial services, primarily savings and credit, to poor households that do not have access to formal financial institutions. At the same time, significant differences of opinion emerged between the supporters of the microfinance movement and various critics, who have become increasingly vocal.

The embrace of microfinance by the mainstream development community is exemplified by the establishment in 1995 of the Consultative Group to Assist the Poorest (CGAP), a multi-donor effort initiated by the World Bank to increase systematically the resources devoted to microfinance.

CGAP now has almost 30 members, comprising international financial institutions and multi-lateral development agencies, as well as bilateral donor agencies. These agencies have pledged resources to support sustainable microfinance in accordance with "best practice" principles agreed by the group.

Subsequently, the popularity of the microfinance movement reached new heights, indeed an apotheosis; with the Micro Credit Summit in Washington, DC in February 1997. The Summit was attended by some 1500 organizations from 137 countries, including a number of heads of state. It launched an ambitious nine-year campaign to reach 100 million of the world's poorest families, and especially the women of those families, with credit for self-employment and other financial and business services by 2005.

The Micro Credit Summit saw microfinance (or more particularly micro-credit) as having enormous potential for reducing poverty. The Micro-Credit Summit further argued that micro-credit had the potential to help most of the world's billion poorest people, based on the following seven findings from practical experience and evaluative studies:

1. Very poor people are a good credit risk, especially in the context of mutual responsibility systems.
2. Sustainability of programs in the developing world is achievable.
3. Micro-credit models have exhibited a high level of replicability.
4. Programs grow to serve large numbers of very poor people.
5. Micro-credit programs help borrowers work their way out of poverty.
6. Micro-credit programs stimulate savings and asset accumulation among poor people.
7. Micro-credit programs become vehicles for a variety of desirable social developments.

This scenario envisages a "win-win" situation, where MFIs cannot only have a major impact in the fight against poverty, but can do so on a sustainable basis without the need for ongoing subsidization.

Indian scenario

Self-Help Group (SHG) model is most prominent in India. It has some similarities with the village bank model, but is less structured. SHGs have around 20 members, most of whom are women. They are based primarily on the principle of lending to their members' savings, but also seek external funding to augment these resources. The SHGs themselves determine the terms and conditions of loans to members. A number of non-government organizations (NGOs) specialize in promoting and motivating SHGs, but the goal is for SHGs to become autonomous institutions. Some NGOs operate as financial intermediaries, while others confine themselves to social intermediation, seeking to link SHGs to regulated banks or other funding agencies. The SHG model is well suited to combining microfinance with other interventions in areas such as health and education, but the relatively loose structure makes it harder to increase outreach quickly and to maintain high standards of performance. On the average, women have proved to be more regular at repayment and commitment. Despite several problems and hurdles, there are many success stories in India through microfinance.

Almost 35 per cent of the women in India are surviving economic crises for long years silently. There are several hurdles that hinder and their dreams remain mere dreams. Hurdles like age-old customs, traditions, culture, religious practices, etc., restrain them to be progressive.

Indian women and literacy

Literacy rates in India are very low. National Literacy Mission (NLM) statistics show that only 54.16 per cent of women are literate. The Commission also lists out factors responsible for poor female literacy rate. Historically, a variety of factors have been found to be responsible for poor female literacy rate, viz.,

1. Gender based inequality.
2. Social discrimination and economic exploitation.
3. Occupation of girl child in domestic chores.
4. Low enrolment of girls in schools.
5. Low retention rate and high dropout rate.

Literacy helps developing entrepreneurial spirit in women. Participation of women in literacy campaigns has opened several opportunities for neo-literate women to step out of the households and involve themselves in some enterprise or a new vocation. The Dumka campaign in Bihar has demonstrated how literacy campaign helped women to take charge of their own lives. They have formed a group called "*Jago Behna*" (Awake Sister), which tries to sensitize the women to the need of collective action against social ills. These women have also set up "*Didi Bank*" (Sister Bank) which promotes the habits of thrift and savings.

Women have also learnt maintaining a hand pump thereby breaking their dependence for repairs on mechanics from outside the village. It also helps them to achieve financial strength and access to credit. In almost all the districts, the literacy campaigns have gone beyond the transaction of mere literary skills and have served to enhance knowledge and skills for better management of expenditure and improving earning capacities. In several districts, the women participants in literacy campaigns have begun to set aside their earnings not only in regular banks but also in specially thrift societies. Such societies, as for example in Dumka are run by the women themselves.

It is the unity and determination of these women that made this drive agrand success. Women at Dumka realized that being in a group or community is always fruitful than being a lone soldier. The power of networking is in its convergence. The convergence of ideas, thoughts, motivation, and fight will always end up in the convergence of benefits. And networking is what would solve the evil. Networking helps the change to happen gradually but steadily and in an ever increasing way in concentric circles. Networking would help women to be in touch with others similarly placed and share ideas, techniques, exchange information and help each other. Globally empowerment of women and gender equality is recognized as a key element to achieve progress in all areas.

Self-Help Groups (SHGs)

The Self-Help Groups (SHGs) predominantly in Andhra Pradesh and elsewhere, aim to do exactly this. Poor rural men and women are given micro-credit to undertake entrepreneurial activity thus helping them generate income and pay back to the bank in small installments. The interest rates are flexible and low and ensure that the women keep something off the income as savings reducing their dependence on banks. Sometimes small groups of women are given credit in groups.

Many more examples exist where private initiatives have made it possible for women to rise out of the poverty and dependence on males in the family or society for livelihood. Feminist empowerment paradigm: underlies the gender policies of many NGOs and the perspectives of some of the consultants and researchers looking at gender impact of microfinance programmes (e.g., Johnson, 1997). This paradigm did not originate as a Northern imposition. It is rooted in the development of some of the earliest microfinance programmes in the South, particularly SEWA and WWF in India. Here the underlying concerns are gender equality and women's human rights. Microfinance is promoted as an entry point in the context of a wider strategy for women's economic and socio-political empowerment. The focus here is on gender awareness and feminist organization. Some programmes have developed very effective means for integrating gender awareness into programmes and for organizing women and men to challenge and change gender discrimination. Some also have legal rights support for women and engage in gender advocacy. *Lizzat Papad* is one such example where women working in a network have been able to make a difference not only in their life but also to the society. It is more beneficial when women operate in a network because it is not just a louder voice but a strengthened workforce, better management, faster access and to summarize adds more gun powder to the equation. *Lizzat Papad* stands a testimony to how networking can be a solution to many problems of women entrepreneurs. Seven women gathered on the terrace of the building and started a small inconspicuous function. The function ended shortly, the result—production of 4 packets of *Papads* and a firm resolve to continue production. This pioneer batch of 7 women had set the ball rolling. As the days went by, the additions to this initial group of 7 was ever-increasing. The institution began to grow. The early days were not easy. The institution had its trials and tribulations. The faith and patience of the members were put to test on several occasions—they had no money but started on a borrowed sum of Rs. 80. Self-reliance was the policy and no monetary help was to be sought (not even voluntarily offered donations). Work, however, started on commercial footing. With quality consciousness as the principle that guided production, Lijjat grew to be the flourishing and successful organization that it is today, a Rs. 300 crore entity. Today Shri Mahila Griha Udyog has a wide range of *papad, khakra, vadi, masala, atta*, bakery products, *chapati, appalam* and detergent and the network supports more than 45,000 families.

Another pioneering initiative in this field was by Dr. Parameswara Rao way back in 1967, when even the commercial banks did not enter the arena of rural banking in a big way. Dr Rao, a Ph.D in Nuclear Physics returned from USA foregoing his bright and lucrative job opportunities to start a movement to help poor women in his home town in Anakapalle district near Vizag, Andhra Pradesh. His wife and other family members stood solidly behind this bold initiative. Dr. Rao could be considered a pioneer in India in what is today called Microfinance to empower women for undertaking income generating and employment creating activities in rural areas. Under the name of 'Bhagavathula Charitable Trust', Dr. Rao started financing women with an aim to providing them livelihood and thereby empowering them to change their status in the society.

As a part of Indian Dairy revolution called the 'Operation Flood', winner of the prestigious Magsaysay Award, *Mrs. Ela Bhatt,* highlighted the need for giving women their due place in dairy development. For their empowerment and economic well-being, women's access to training in modern dairying and cooperative management is essential.

The employment of women is an index of their economic and social status in society. In India, women constitute 90 per cent of marginal workers, with some regional variations.

The Operation Flood (OF) program recognizes that:

- Dairying at the household level is largely the domain of women.
- The products and income from dairying can be controlled by women.
- Dairying can be practiced on a small scale.

The prevailing dairy scenario presents many dilemmas.

- The first one is that modern dairying is geared to maximum production as opposed to traditional subsistence dairying.
- The second is that an expanding national herd of milch and other animals is dependent on diminishing and degrading common property resources for grazing and crop residues and other biomass.

- The third is traditional dairying is largely dominated by men. All these have to be resolved within the framework of sustainable development.

The membership in most of India's 70,000 village-level dairy cooperative societies (DCS) is heavily dominated by men. The picture is now gradually changing in the favor of women. Efforts are on to give them their due place in dairy development. Presently, some 2,476 all-woman DCS are functioning in the country in selected states. Out of 9.2 million total memberships in DCS, 1.63 million are women (18%). However, women constitute less than three per cent of total board members.

Another such organization dedicated to the upliftment of the status of women and strive towards the financial empowerment of women is SEWA. Self Employment Women Association (SEWA) is a trade union registered in 1972. It is an organization of poor, self-employed women workers. These are women who earn a living through their own labour or small businesses. They do not obtain regular salaried employment with welfare benefits like workers in the organized sector. They are the unprotected labour force of our country. Constituting 93 per cent of the labour force, these are workers of the unorganized sector. Of the female Labour force in India, more than 94 per cent are in the unorganized sector. However, their work is not counted and hence remains invisible. In fact, women workers themselves remain uncounted, undercounted and invisible.

SEWA is an organization of 158,000 women workers in Gujarat in western India. Its experience in the arid zone of Banaskantha district has shown that among the many inputs, fodder is the key to milk production. This could also become part of the larger program of ecological restoration. All the defunct primary societies in Radhanpur and Santhalpur talukas of the district were revived, strengthened and consolidated. By self-reliance we mean that women should be autonomous and self-reliant, individually and collectively, both economically and in terms of their decision-making ability. At SEWA workers are organized to achieve their goals of full employment and self reliance through the strategy of struggle and development. In relation to 'Operation Flood' Earlier, SEWA used to provide the revolving fund for the purpose. Now, 35 per cent of the investment is being done by women themselves.

In some talukas, SEWA is also harvesting and helping in drinking water supply. Additional employment is generated through home-based craft with assured marketing. In 1995, the total sales amounted to Rs. 9 million. The integrated approach of organizing the rural women into their own economic bodies like Dairy Cooperatives, Savings and Credit Groups, labor unions and DWACRA Association has stabilized the families in their own homeland (migration has declined by about 80 per cent), regenerating their local ecology, and added income and assets worth Rs. 30 million.

Gandhian thinking is the guiding force for SEWA's poor, self-employed members in organizing for social change. They follow the principles of *satya* (truth), *ahimsa* (non-violence), *sarvadharma* (integrating all faiths, all people) and *khadi* (propagation of local employment and self reliance). SEWA is both an organization and a movement. The SEWA movement is enhanced by its being a *sangam* or confluence of three movements: the Labour movement, the cooperative movement and the women's movement. But it is also a movement of self-employed workers: their own, home-grown movement with women as the leaders. Through their own movement, women become strong and visible. Their tremendous economic and social contributions thus become recognized.

A majority of microfinance programs target women with the explicit goal of empowering them. However, their underlying premises are different. Some argue that women are amongst the poorest and the most vulnerable of the underprivileged. Others believe that investing in women's capabilities empowers them to make choices, which is valuable in itself, and also contributes to greater economic growth and development. Another motivation is the evidence from literature that shows that an increase in woman's resources result in higher well-being of the family, especially children. Finally, an increasing number of microfinance institutions prefer women members as they believe that they are better and more reliable borrowers thereby contributing to their financial viability.

A more feminist point of view stresses that access to financial resources presents an opportunity for greater empowerment of women. Though many agree that women empowerment is an important development objective for microfinance programs, it is still unclear what women empowerment means. Additional services like training, awareness raising workshops and other activities over and above the minimalist (financial services only) microfinance approach are also an important determinant of the degree of its impact on the empowerment process of women. So several steps need to be taken to provide more information and access to information to women at all levels to make good use of the microfinance and the opportunities it provides. Only then sustainable empowerment is possible. This would be a long term approach rather than a short one.

Suggestions

According to Mrs. Ela Bhatt, the poor rural households need a whole package of supporting inputs and services to develop dairying as an effective instrument of household livelihood. However, as the experience goes, these inputs are not always easily accessible to poor, rural women. Major factors that hamper the success of women's cooperatives are:

Resistance to women as cooperative members: Women are yet to be recognized as farmers in their own right. In a mixed cooperative, lack of ownership of land prevents women not only from becoming member but also from obtaining credit, training, technical assistance. Women also do not have any say in the decision-making policies of the cooperatives and thus cannot help formulate more policies to help themselves. Concrete strategies have to be devised to help women get ownership and control over productive assets, individually and collectively. It will be the single most important factor towards their empowerment and economic well-being. Some of these assets include a plot of land, housing, workshed, animals and shareholding of cooperatives.

- *Low literacy*
- *Resistance* from the upper socio-economic section of village community towards the poor.
- *Access to finance (lack of):* Small-farm household women need timely finance (credit) for short-term investments to manage their dairy enterprises in an efficient manner. For example, they cannot meet the needs of cattle feed, fodder and other essential inputs without ready cash. Facilities should also be made available for timely breeding of dairy animals and health care. A World Bank study of the project benefits in villages of Madhya Pradesh suggests that the lack of credit for the initial purchase of dairy animals remains a major constraint to OF's ability to reach the poorest households.
- *Access to training facilities (lack of):* Women should be imparted training in dairy husbandry, cooperative management and marketing. There is also a need for social organization at the pre-cooperative stage to help in the formation of cooperatives as well as dissemination of the economics of dairy activity.

The positive change that microfinance has brought to the life of women is impressive. Still there are several things that it can achieve. They are:

1. Ensure that the initiatives started with the help of microfinance achieve sustainability stage.

2. Continuously encourage exchange of information related to financial, market-oriented trends so that women have a competitive edge over other players in the market.
3. Provide technological know how and help to move them from one stage to the other in the knowledge economy and the market chain.
4. A multi-pronged approach to ensure each empowered women changes the life of another and shift the living standards of the families.
5. Empowerment is an ongoing process, hence needs constant encouragement and should spread like a viral movement across societies which would work as a network.

An empowerment approach does, however, involve a significant change in attitude and work practices and the challenging of vested interests. Flexibility to women's needs and deciding the best ways of combining empowerment and sustainability objectives can only be achieved on the basis of extensive consultation with women, research on their needs, strategies and constraints, and a process of negotiation between women and development agencies. It therefore inevitably requires a more comprehensive framework for women's participation at all levels, rather than imposition of particular models depending on the particular donor fashion extant at the time.

Finally, despite the potential contribution of microfinance programmes to women's empowerment, realizing this contribution is dependent on, rather than a substitute for, adequate welfare provision and feminist mobilization. What is particularly worrying about the current situation is that financially sustainable minimalist microfinance is being promoted as the key strategy for poverty alleviation and empowerment in response to ever-decreasing official development assistance budgets. Unless microfinance is conceived as part of a broader strategy for transformation of gender inequality, it risks becoming yet one more means of shifting the costs and responsibilities for development onto very poor women.

It works, because it supports the strengths of these women. It supports their self-help efforts.

REFERENCES

1. *Micro Credit For Women in Rural Bangladesh: Retrenchment of Patriarchal Hegemony as a Consequence*, by Rahman Aminur, Chicago Anthropology Exchange.
2. *Gender Empowerment in Microfinance* by Beatriz Armendáriz, Harvard University, UCL, and CERMi (Université Libre de Bruxelles).
3. *Credit for Alleviation of Rural Poverty: Institute Research Report*, Hossain, Mahabub, February. Washington, D.C: International Food Policy Research.
4. The concept of the informal sector was introduced in a paper by Keith Hart, "Informal Income Opportunities and the Structure of Urban Unemployment in Ghana," paper presented at a conference on Urban Unemployment in Africa, University of Sussex, 1971.
5. Elisabeth Rhyne and Maria Otero, "Financial Services for Micro enterprises: Principles and Institutions," in Maria Otero and Elisabeth Rhyne, eds., *The New World of Micro enterprise Finance* (West Hartford: Kumarian Press, 1994).
6. World Bank, *World Development Report 2007.*
7. I. Getubig, J. Remenyi and B. Quinones, eds., *Creating the Vision: Micro financing the Poor in Asia-Pacific,* Kuala Lumpur: Asian and Pacific Development Centre,1997.
8. Jonathan Morduch, "The Microfinance Promise," *Journal of Economic Literature*, Vol. 37 (December 1999).
9. Asian Development Bank, *Microfinance Development Strategy,* Manila: ADB, 1999.
10. *Microfinance and women's empowerment: Rethinking 'best practice'* Linda Mayoux.

11. *Micro-Finance and the Empowerment of Women*, Linda Mayoux.
12. "Microfinance and the Empowerment of Women", The Fourth World Conference on Women, Baijing, 1995.
13. "Financing Microenterprises: An analytical study of Islamic Microfinance institutions" by Habib Ahmed, *Journal of Islamic Economic Studies*.

Websites:

1. www.freedomfromhunger.org
2. www.gfusa.org
3. http://povlibrary.worldbank.org/files/14648_Grameen-web.pdf
4. http://www.uncdf.org/english/microfinance/facts.php
5. http://www.gemconsortium.org/download/1232428620182/GEM_Global_08.pdf
6. http://www.fiwe.org/index.php?option=com_frontpage&Itemid=137
7. http://www.lijjat.com/
8. http://awakeindia.org.in/main.php
9. http://www.fiwe.org/
10. http://www.gendercide.org
11. http://www.census.gov/

4

Role of Self-Help Groups in India

*Dr. Y. Subbarayudu
**Dr. G. Haranath

Introduction

Mohammed Yunus of Chittagong University, a Nobel Prize winner of Bangladesh popularized the concept of Self-Help Group (SHG). SHG is a group of rural poor who have volunteered to organise themselves into a group for eradication of poverty of the members. They agree to save regularly and convert their savings into a Common Fund known as the Group corpus. They use this common fund and such other funds that they may receive as a group through a common management.

A SHG is a small group of persons who come together with the intention of finding a solution to a common problem such as medical issues, livelihood generation or watershed management, with a degree of self-sufficiency. Generally a self-help group may consist of 10 to 20 persons. All members of the group should belong to families below the poverty line

* M.Com., M.B.A., Ph.D., Assistant Professor, Department of M.B.A., Yogi Vemana University, Kadapa, Andhra Pradesh

** M.Com., M.B.A., M.F.T., M.F.M., Ph.D., Assistant Professor, Department of Commerce, Yogi Vemana University, Kadapa, Andhra Pradesh.

(BPL). However, if necessary, a maximum of 20 per cent and in exceptional cases, where essentially required, up to a maximum of 30 per cent of the members in a group may be taken from families marginally above the poverty line (APL). This will help the families of occupational groups like agricultural labourers, marginal farmers and artisans marginally above the poverty line, or who may have been excluded from the BPL list to become members of the Self Help Group. However, the above poverty line members will not be eligible for the subsidy under the scheme.

The SHG should devise a code of conduct (Group management norms) to bind itself. The members should build their corpus through regular savings. The group should develop financial management norms covering the loan sanction procedure, repayment schedule and interest rates. The members in the group meetings should take all the loaning decisions through a participatory decision-making process. The group should be able to prioritise the loan applications, fix repayment schedules, fix appropriate rate of interest for the loans advanced and closely monitor the repayment of the loan installments from the loaned. The group should operate a group account preferably in their service area bank branch, so as to deposit the balance amounts left with the group after disbursing loans to its members.

Andhra Pradesh is one of the pioneer states in encouraging SGHs. It is doing well in this aspect. Impressed by the remarkable success of women self-help groups (SHGs) in Andhra Pradesh, the World Bank has said that the model could be replicated in other states in India and in other countries. With more than 6,00,000 SHGs now operating in Andhra Pradesh, covering 87 per cent of the state's rural poor, the women's silent revolution is all set to unleash a storm of change.

The state of Andhra Pradesh has used development of SHGs extensively as a primary tool of poverty alleviation and empowerment. National and state government initiatives, as well as NGO efforts, have used SHGs to implement poverty alleviation programs in Andhra Pradesh since 1979. Early programs sought to provide self-employment, empower, and incorporate rural poor women into the development process. Homogenous groups of women would choose and collectively undertake an economic activity suited to their skills and resources, supplemented by state matching grants. Following on successes in earlier programs, which were modified to make them more meaningful, the state has promoted significant increases in SHGs using a social mobilization approach.

The state-sponsored *Velugu* program working in over 860 mandals in 22 districts, aims to reach 2.9 million of the poorest of rural poor. Both the number and structure of SGHs in Andhra Pradesh has been scaled up. The state established an independent support organization to implement poverty elimination projects, which aim at social mobilization to enhance livelihoods and employment generation opportunities of the poor. Self-managed grassroots institutions have been federated into village level and sub-district level groups. These groups provide an organizational identity to help SHGs realize the benefits of a larger organization without losing the advantages of small organization. Federations of SHGs are fast becoming powerful voices expressing the social and economic needs of the poor. Capacity building is an important component in the scaling up of Andhra Pradesh's poverty alleviation initiatives.

Andhra Pradesh has chosen social mobilization and inclusiveness as methods of addressing poverty alleviation. The process uses social mobilization as an institutional mechanism to help the poor interact with government machinery so that public resources and services are better accessed. To insure that the 'poor' were adequately identified, and thus included, the community itself prepares a list of its poor people. The participatory methodology of identifying the poor has been very effective in creating a transparent and inclusive methodology for community based targeting for programs. Besides group mobilization, the programs focus on expanding the assets of the poor and creating economic opportunities connected with people's livelihoods. To reduce, mitigate and manage risk *Velugu* supports the Community Investment Fund which supports investments in sub-projects for the poor and the Comprehensive Insurance Package which seeks to develop a community-based delivery of life and health insurance services.

Present scenario of SHGs

A number of social issues including gender and family, child labor, disability and health related to poverty alleviation need to be addressed in the context of SHGs. SHG formations largely take place around women since women are seen as more credit-worthy than men. But the process of empowerment and poverty alleviation can be more sustainable when all the members of the family are involved. Hence women's groups are taken as an entry point for the formation of men's groups, youth groups, children groups, and groups for the physically challenged.

There is absolutely no doubt that SHGs have lead to an expansion in the economic spaces of members. However the composition of the members reveals that the coverage of the poor is low, while the coverage of non-poor is considerable. The financial status of households and savings capacities has improved due to improvement in access to formal credit institutions, since SHGs are linked with banks. Access to credit has enabled women to undertake economic activities, which tend to be an expansion or strengthening of existing traditional activities. A smaller proportion of women have taken up new occupations. The diversification of occupation to non-agricultural activities has enhanced the quality of income of the households by reducing the dependency on risk-based agriculture. Increases in income have been spent on better nutrition for the children and on health care for the family. Kitchen gardens have enhanced the overall nutritional status of children, pregnant and lactating mothers. Social inclusion and participation in the political process are also impacted by SHGs. Gender poverty measured in terms of gender bias with respect to norms of eating, male preference in distribution of food and access to clothing has not declined significantly. But food security of member households improved after participation in groups. There are improvements in school enrolment, attendance, drainage facilities, toilet facilities and access to electricity and gas. The political process picks up momentum with the SHGs being federated and also establishing links with local self-governing bodies. Further, SHGs have the capacity to voice the needs of the communities. There is tremendous potential in this endeavor if the vision of SHGs is expanded beyond transacting money to include local concerns about the quality of life.

Accountability is a must for any program to succeed. The most obvious relationship of accountability and transparency is between the state and the people. Both have to be accountable to each other. This requires a system of communication where intent, need and impact of programs can be conveyed both ways. In Andhra Pradesh, the linkages between different approaches towards development, poverty reduction and empowerment must be considered. It is not enough to address the economic indicators of poverty. While incomes have to be augmented through livelihood generation interventions, for which credit is an important component, determinants of human poverty in terms of health and education requirements require attention. Likewise, social poverty, which manifests in the presence of corrosive evils like caste taboos, norms of dowry, adherence to vices such as alcohol and drugs have to be woven into empowerment programs.

Self-Help groups' political potential is powerful. Federations form the training ground to make leaders and potential political aspirants. This critical mass has tremendous potential to work for the betterment of the regions they represent. The potential of women-only SHGs for women's empowerment depends upon several other supportive measures like education, health, housing and infrastructure. Partnerships are fundamental for development. This kind of inclusiveness where institutions and actors both public and private, work in synergy, has considerable potential for poverty alleviation. Market dynamics are not adequate to allocate costs and benefits. It is however difficult to conclusively say what the effect of excluding NGOs will be. In a larger design of partnerships, it may not be advisable to create rifts between actors working towards similar goals

The linkage between the national, regional and local environment can be made with political will. Unless a sense of ownership is infused into any program, participants will not demand accountability or feel accountable. Involving people at every level of decision making within the program transforms 'beneficiaries' into participants and ultimately everyone benefits. A complex mix of methods is needed to solve complicated problems such as poverty. Use of existing structures and the creation of new edifices have to be synchronized. Economic and social issues are equally important if poverty is to be understood.

Suggestions for strengthening of SHGs

SHGs should be strengthened further to achieve the targeted objectives. The following suggestions may help in this regard.

1. There must be a monitoring cell appointed by the state government with its wings at all district headquarters, to look into the affairs of SGHs. Without interfering much, it should help the SGHs in case of any trouble.
2. The government should ensure full protection to the SGH members from the village moneylenders and other anti-social elements. This is because; the scheme is a loss to such people and their businesses.

3. The prorogation about the scheme should be a continuous one. This may create awareness among the rural women masses.
4. The government should take all possible steps to literate rural women, which directly helps SHGs to strengthen further.
5. It is also the duty of the state government to supply matching grants to SHGs without any delay as and when they are due.

REFERENCES

1. Ananta Basudev Sahu and Sandhya Rani Das—Research article on *Women Empowerment Thorough Self Help Groups-A Case Study.*
2. Tiyas Biswas, *Women Empowerment Through Microfinance: A Boon for Development*—a research article.
3. Ashok Kumari, *Development of Women and Children in India*, Common Wealth Publishers, New Delhi, 1990.
4. Thomas Fisher and M.S. Sriram, *Beyond micro-credit putting development back into microfinance*, Vistaar Publications, New Delhi, 2004.
5. http://www.techno-preneur.net
6. http:/www.smallindustryindia.com
7. http://www.nabard.org/roles/mcid/shgbanklink.htm
8. http://www.newdelhi.mfa.no/Development+Cooperation/Default.htm#Women

5

Microfinance through SHG for Poverty Alleviation in Arunachal Pradesh

*Debabrata Maji

ABSTRACT

Creating self employment opportunities is one way of attacking poverty and solving the problems of unemployment. Microfinance is the effective tools for rural masses. There are over 24 crore people below the poverty line in the country. The Scheme of Micro-Credit has been found as an effective instrument for lifting the poor above the level of poverty by providing them increased self-employment opportunities and making them credit worthy. Total requirement of micro-credit in the country has been assessed at Rs. 50,000 crore. Micro-credit programme works through NGOs/SHGs and the merit lies in weekly monitoring and refund of installments. The rate of recovery under SIDBI's Micro-credit programme is as high as 98 per cent. Though there are various departments and organizations implementing micro-credit schemes in the areas of activity falling under their purview but their total reach is

* Centre for Appropriate Technology and Rural Development, North Eastern Regional Institute of Science and Technology, Nirjuli (Itanagar), Arunachal Pradesh.

very low, i.e. not more than Rs. 5,000 crore. Thus, the existing programme caters to only 5 to 10 per cent of total requirements and there is considerable scope for expansion of such programme. An attempt has been made to showcase the success story of Microfinance programme in Arunachal Pradesh with constraint and challenges and integrated holistic approach to gear up towards poverty alleviation.

Introduction

There are nearly 100 crore poor people who have no access to formal financial services in the world, out of which 20 per cent live in India. Microfinance defined for providing credit, thrift and finance related services and products of very small amount to improve the living standards of poor and the downtrodden. In India, loans up to Rs. 25,000 are covered under Microfinance. A good number of small enterprises could be survived with these social-oriented entrepreneurial activities. The concept is to make the poor are bankable and the micro-enterprise finance through repayment incentive structure, streamlined the administration and market-based pricing adopting profit centre approach. This approach leads to major changes in a cumulative cause triggered by credit to rural masses as well as Small and Medium Enterprises (SMEs) to the ultimate benefit of rural economy. Md. Yunus founder of Grameen Bank in Bangladesh and pioneer in micro-credit said that one can run a bank by mobilizing low cost deposit; lending money and getting it back after covering all costs and make a profit resulting in eradication of poverty and unemployment. Microfinance provides a wide range of financial services to the poor on a sustainable basis slowly but steadily gaining popularity. Microfinance service is provided primarily through the following:

- *Formal institutions:* Regional Rural Bank, Cooperatives
- *Semi-formal institutions:* Non-Government Organizations

- *Informal sources:* Moneylenders and Shopkeepers.

As far as rural economy is concerned, agriculture contributes more than 20 per cent of GDP and provides 57 per cent employment to country's workforce and ensures livelihood support to nearly 2/3rd of country's growing population. Agricultural activities support rural economy through both backward and forward linkages. Micro-financing is to focus on economically active poor sectors so that there is no downward migration for them. In the broader sense, the aim of microfinance is to develop habits with financial vision among the rural poor, so that they are able to save, seek credit and know several finance related aspects to improve their financial position and living standards. The focus of microfinance is to facilitate the shift from induced development from the above to initiated development from below. The vast potential and opportunities of Microfinance in India are yet to be fully tapped. As per the 10th Plan document, 26 per cent of the population lives below the poverty line, out of which 19.3 per cent in the rural and the remaining 6.7 per cent in urban areas. Thus, there is primarily demand for the microfinance support which is generally met by commercial banks, co-operative banks including rural banks. Free market economic principles can change the lives of the poor people. Microfinance is growing very rapidly and due attention from banks, financial institutions, Non-Government Organizations (NGOs) and the Government is needed. A vibrant and developed microfinance sector would impact economic development across the country and wealth among the populous for ultimately narrowing down the gap between the haves and have-nots. Commercial banks adopted new concepts of Micro-Credit, formation of Self-Help Groups and credit linking with a view to minimize the transaction cost in rural lending. Besides low intermediation cost, these strategies have twin advantages of high recovery rate and higher frequency of recycling of funds. Cohesive group and peer pressure are the intrinsic strength of the micro-financing activities through SHG.

Micro-Credit

Satyamurti and Haokip (2002) said Micro-credit serves best those who have identified an economic opportunity and who are in a position to capitalize on that opportunity if they are provided with a small amount of ready cash. Thus, the poor those are worked in stable or growing economies have demonstrated an ability to undertake the proposed activities in an entrepreneurial manner and have demonstrated a commitment to repay their debts (instead of feeling that the credit represents some form of social-vindication), are the best candidates for micro-credit. In order to appreciate the phenomenal success of micro-credit, it would be proper to look into the principles on which it works. These principles are valid for all types of micro-credit.

- Poverty is not created by the poor, but by the institutions and policies which surround them. In order to eliminate poverty, appropriate changes have to be made in these institutions or policies. Alternatively, new ones have to be created.
- Charity is not an answer to poverty. It serves only to perpetuate poverty and create dependency. It takes away the initiative of an individual to break through the wall of poverty. The way to overcome poverty is to unleash the energy and creativity in each human being.
- There is no difference in the ability of a poor person than any other person. The poor does not got the opportunity to explore their potential and their abilities remain unutilized or underutilized. If they had the opportunity, they would be able to change their own lives.
- Micro-credit is based on the principle different from the banking principles. Conventional banks start with the principle that the more you have, the more you can get which provides a springboard for those who

are already well off. The Micro-credit works on the principle, the less the person has, the higher the priority she gets.

- Poor people always payback.
- Lending to women brings greater benefits to the family than lending to man. If the mother is the borrower, the children are the immediate beneficiaries. Women have greater long-term vision and are ready to bring about changes in their lives step by step. They are excellent managers of scarce resources.

The Self-Help Group

It is in the background of failure of banks to reach the poor that the idea of Self-Help Groups (SHGs) began to take shape. A SHG is a group of about 10 to 20 persons from homogeneous background who come together for addressing the common problems. They collect voluntary savings on a regular basis and use the pooled resources to make small interest bearing loans to their members. At a later stage, these groups are able to obtain credit from outside sources to support income generating activities. Very often, there is a self-help promoting institution (SHPI), which enables the SHGs to function effectively. The evolution of SHGs could be traced at three levels:

- At the first level, households use microfinance to meet 'survival' requirements where small savings and loans serve as a buffer in the event of emergency or to smooth consumption or even to service previous debt or to give itself more liquidity during lean times.
- At the second level 'subsistence' needs are met through microfinance, where a household begins to utilize microfinance to diversify its basket of income generating activities or to meet working capital requirements for traditional activities.

- At the third level, as the households reach a stage where they can assume a higher degree of risk, microfinance could be used to invest in setting up an enterprises or facilitating entry into employment in one way or the other household becomes 'sustainable'.

SHG is a micro organization. So, it have the entire essential features of a good organization, e.g. organizational management, financial management etc. It is preferred by all the members of an SHG belong to the same socio-economic background having common interests, needs and objectives. The group should preferably be homogenous in terms of socio-economic condition, age, sex, place and occupation. The group should also have affinity in terms of common interest, like-mindedness, and mutual support and understanding, concern for each other, faith and trust etc. SHG is a micro democratic unit where each member has to express her or himself freely and participate effectively in decision-making or other proceedings. The SHGs are informal bodies and need not necessarily be registered. However, the SHG will have a name, an identity, rules and regulations, necessary records etc.

SHG challenges

It is generally accepted that SHG often do not include the poorest of the poor due to:

- *Social factors*: The poorest are often those who are socially marginalized because of caste affiliation and those who are most skeptical of the potential benefits of collective action.
- *Economic factors:* The poorest often do not have the financial resources to contribute to the savings and pay membership fees; they are often the ones who migrate during the lean season, thus making group membership difficult).
- *Intrinsic biases of the implementing organizations*: As the poorest of the poor are the most difficult to

reach and motivate, implementing agencies tend to leave them out, preferring to focus on the next wealth category).

Efforts have to made to overcome this bias, e.g. through participatory wealth ranking at the community level, or by using indices to identify the poorest. Simanowitz et al. (1999) suggested for active poverty target, which is required to include the poorest in microfinance programs. But including them in SHGs is not enough, which need to be design in such a way that realistic investment opportunities for poorest households exist. Once SHG are established and start saving, they generally attempt to gain access to larger amounts of capital in order to broaden the range of micro-enterprises available to them.

SHG and Bank

SHG may sustain in the rural economy if group members have access to financial capital and markets for their products and services. The groups initially generate their own savings through thrift to link up with financial institutions in order to obtain further loans for investments in rural enterprises. NGOs and banks are giving loans to SHGs either as "matching loans" (proportionate to the group's savings) or as fixed amounts, depending on the group's record of repayment, recommendations by group facilitators, collaterals provided, etc. Wilson (2002) estimated that there are 500,000 SHGs in India, with a membership of 8 million people, who are linked to about 20,000 rural outlets of more than 440 banks, with an advance portfolio of more than 240 million dollar.

Satyamurti and Haokip (2002) said microfinance has been defined by the taskforce on Microfinance constituted by the National Bank for Agriculture and Rural Development (NABARD) as provision of thrift, credit and other financial services and products of very small amounts to the poor to enable them to raise their income and improve their living standards. The upper limit of amount is fixed at Rs. 25,000 under microfinance programme. Table 5.1 shows the comparative analysis of Microfinance services available to poor.

SHG Surveillance

Self-Help Groups mobilize savings from their members and lend these funds to one another with high rate of interest. This high returns may be invested in their micro-enterprises, or even higher cost of funds from moneylenders. If they do not wish to use the money, they may deposit the same in bank. If the members need funds exceeds the groups accumulated savings, they may borrow from a bank or other organization as a microfinance NGO. The system is very flexible. The group aggregates the small individual saving and borrowing requirements of its members, and the bank needs only to maintain one account for the group as a single entity. The banker must assess the competence and integrity of the group as a micro-bank, but once it has done this need not concern with the individual loans. The Bank may treat the group as a single customer, those total business and transactions are probably similar to the average normal customers as they represent the combined banking business of some twenty 'micro-customers'. Unlike many customers, demand from SHGs is not price-sensitive. Illiterate village women are sometimes better bankers than the professional qualified. They know that rapid access to funds is more important than their cost although they are unable to calculate the figures. The typical micro-enterprise earns over 500 per cent return on the small sum invested in it (Harper, 1998). Thus, the groups charges high rates of interest and happy to take advantage of the generous spread. The NABARD subsidized bank lending rate of 12 per cent allows them, but they are also willing to borrow from NGO/MFIs or lend funds from SIDBI at 15 per cent or Grameen Bank (private) at 18.5 per cent or 21 per cent.

Table 5.1: Comparative analysis of microfinance services available to poor

Parameter	Moneylender	Commercial Banks	Govt. Sponsored Programme	Financial Products of MFIs
Ease to access	High	Low	Low	High
Transaction cost of access	Low	Very high	Very high	Low-medium
Lead time for loans	Very short	Extremely long	Extremely long	Short
Repayment terms	Fixed and rigid	Fixed and easy	Extremely long	Flexible
Interest rates	Exorbitantly high	Low and very affordable	Low, affordable and subsidized	Reasonable and affordable
Incentives	None	None	None	Repeat and large loans, interest rebates
Repeat borrowing	Possible	Possible but not likely	Extremely long	Stream of credit is assured
Loan access procedures	Very quick	Extremely time consuming and complicated	Extremely time consuming and complicated	Simple and quick
Loan application procedures	Informal but exploitative	Exhaustive and complex	Exhaustive and complex	Simple and informal
Collateral and demand promissory note	Mandatory	Required but hypothecation of asset may suffice	Not required although a charge on the asset becomes automatic	Not required—social collateral is used for physical collateral

Source: R. Arunachalam

Role of NABARD

The NABARD led Self-Help Group (SHG)-Bank Linkage Programme in rural areas, with credit linkage of 2 million SHGs by December 2005, as the largest and fastest growing microfinance programme of the world, is a major breakthrough achieved by the banks in last few years. A stimulus to the rapid growth of SHGs was provided when SHG-bank linkage programme was initiated in 1992. It was a pilot project for promoting 500 SHGs. As the idea gained acceptance from the banking system and the results were promising, the RBI encouraged this positive initiative by issuing instructions to banks in 1996 to cover SHG financing as a mainstream activity under the priority sector lending portfolio. The Working Group headed by Shri S. K. Kalia, MD, NABARD was set up by the RBI in 1994 came up with wide ranging recommendations on SHG and bank linkage as a potential innovation in the area of banking with the poor. RBI support has been instrumental in the phenomenal growth of micro-credit under SHGs Banks Linkage Programme. Table 5.2 shows the number of SHGs of NABARD.

Model-1

In this model, the bank itself acts as a Self-Help Group Promoting Institution (SHPI). It takes initiatives in forming the groups, nurtures them over a period of time and then provides credit to them after satisfying itself about their maturity to absorb credit. About 16 per cent of SHGs and 13 per cent of loan amounts are using this model as of March 2002.

Model-2

In this model, groups are formed by NGOs or by government agencies. The groups are nurtured and trained by these agencies. The bank then provides credit directly to the SHGs, after observing their operations and maturity to absorb credit. While the bank provides loans to the groups directly, the

Table 5.2: Growth of SHGs and micro-credit no. of SHGs linked to banks in India

Year	No. of SHGs	Bank Loan (Rs. Crore)
1992-93	255	0.29
1993-94	620	0.65
1994-95	2122	2.45
1995-96	4757	6.06
1996-97	8598	11.84
1997-98	14317	23.76
1998-99	32995	57.07
1999-00	114775	192.98
2000-01	263825	480.90
2001-02	461478	1026.30
2002-03	717360	2048.70
2003-04	1079091	3904.20
2004-05	1628476	6898.46
2005-06	1830000	8319.00

Source: NABARD and Economic Surveys

facilitating agencies continue their interactions with the SHGs. Most linkage experiences begin with this model with NGOs playing a major role. This model has also been popular and more acceptable to banks, as some of the difficult functions of social dynamics are externalized. About 75 per cent of SHGs and 78 per cent of loan amounts are using this model.

Model-3

Due to various reasons, banks in some areas are not in a position to finance SHGs promoted and nurtured by other agencies. In such cases, the NGOs act as both facilitators and microfinance intermediaries. First, they promote the groups, nurture and train them and then approach banks for bulk loans for on-lending to the SHGs. About 9 per cent of SHGs and 13 per cent of loan amounts are using this model.

Role of SIDBI

The success of Micro-credit programme lies in diversification of services. Microfinance Scheme of SIDBI is under operation since January, 1999 with a corpus of Rs. 100 crore and a network of about 190 capacity assessed rated NGOs. Under the programme, total amount of Rs. 191 crore have been sanctioned up to 31st December, 2003, benefiting over 9 lakh beneficiaries. Under the programme, NGOs are supposed to provide equity support in order to avail SIDBI finance. But they find it difficult to manage the needed equity support because of their poor financial condition. The problem has got aggravated due to declining interest rate on deposits. Programme to SIDBI, which shall be called 'Portfolio Risk Fund' (PRF). This fund was used for security deposit of the loan amount from the NGOs and to meet the cost of interest loss. At present, SIDBI takes fixed deposit equal to 10 per cent of the loan amount. The share of NGOs would be 2.5 per cent of the loan amount (i.e. 25% of security deposit) and balance 7.5 per cent (i.e. 75% of security deposit) would be adjusted from the funds provided by the Government of India. The NGOs may avail the loan from the SIDBI for further on lending on the support of the security deposit.

OVERVIEW OF ARUNACHAL PRADESH

Arunachal Pradesh, described as the island of peace, is said to be the fastest developing state today. It is said that within the span of a few decades the people of the state have traversed many centuries. It is the most strategically located state in the extreme north-eastern part of India having an international border with Bhutan on the west, China on the north, Burma on the east and the state of Assam on the south spread over a mountainous territory of Eastern Himalayas over 83,743 sq. km and inhabited by 10.91 lakh people according to 2001 census and is scattered over 17 towns and 3649 villages. Its climate varies from sub-tropical in the south to alpine in the north. Evergreen forests covers more than 60 per cent of the state with its numerous turbulent streams, roaring rivers, deep gorges, lofty mountains, snow-clad shinning peaks, hundreds and thousands of species of flora and fauna. Its endless variation of scenic beauty is the first to great sunrise in the new millennium of the 21st century in the country. Arunachal Pradesh has attained the status of 24th full-fledged state through different stages of political and administrative development in February 20, 1987, thus enabling the people to occupy their rightful place in the Indian Union. Prior to 1947 the British followed the policy of speculation in the tribal area. After Independence the Government of India changed the policy of isolation as applied by the then British. The Constitution of India, which attained its full shape on January 26, 1950, has many provisions for the development of tribal people in India. Before 1962, the area was popularly known as North-East Frontier Agency (NEFA) comprising five districts and was constitutionally a part of Assam. But, because of its strategic importance and the peculiar nature of its problem the Ministry of External Affairs administered it until 1965 and subsequently by the Ministry of Home Affairs, through the Governor of Assam acting on behalf of the President of India. In 1972, it becomes a Union Territory with the name Arunachal Pradesh. In line with the renaming of the territory, the system of political representation was stepped up from a Pradesh Council to a Legislative Assembly (Provisional) in 1975. Council of Ministers was sworn in on August 15, 1975. The first General Election to the Legislative Assembly was held in 1978, consulting a landmark in the political evolution of the state. With the further re-organization of various districts, subsequently for administrative convenience, now there are 17 districts in the state. Zilla Parisads, Anchal Samities and Gram Panchayats at various levels function as advisory bodies for development work. Itanagar is the capital of the state now. It is named after Ita Fort meaning Fort of Bricks.

Development came late to Arunachal Pradesh. For historical reasons the area remained completely unaffected by progress till independence. Even thereafter, when the planning era commenced in 1950, investment in Arunachal Pradesh remained insignificant over the First Five-Year Plans. It was only the 5th plan period onwards that there has been a perceptible step-up in plan allocation.

Microfinance Vision 2011 of Arunachal Pradesh

"Women of Arunachal Pradesh are among the hardest working people of the country taking care of both, the livelihood systems and home management. Economic empowerment of the women is considered critical for healthy and all encompassing growth of the society. Given the limited outreach of the banking system in the state, women, especially the poor women are not in a position to gain access to financial services including savings and credit. The Self-Help Group (SHG) movement of the country is now recognized, by far, the largest microfinance movement of the worlds. Unfortunately, the state has been grossly lagging behind in this area. In order to correct this imbalance and give an opportunity to the poor women of the state to save their frugal resources and put them to productive use by mutual lending, and later on access to large bank resources, it is proposed to give special boost to the promotion of SHGs of women during 2008-09. The state government, with technical support of NABARD and banking system, will promote 5,000 SHGs by 2011 over next three years, of which, 1,500 SHGs will be promoted during 2008-09 to raise income levels of households and improve living standards. This will cover all the poor families of the state under a massive micro-saving movement. The department of Women and Child will be the nodal department. The state government also appointed a senior officers as Microfinance Coordinator." This was stated by Shri Kalikho Pul, Hon'ble Minister (Finance), Govt. of Arunachal Pradesh during his budget speech for the period 2008-09.

NABARD in Arunachal Pradesh

During the past few years of existence in Arunachal Pradesh, NABARD has played a strategic role in overall economic development of the state. NABARD in partnership with established NGOs and state government conducted a numbers of promotional programmes for capacity-building of the rural youths and farmers of the state for taking up various income generating activities, empowerment of women, diversification of agriculture and adoption of modern agriculture practices to strengthen the rural credit delivery system. NABARD has supported 16 Rural Entrepreneurship Development Programme (REDPs) in association with eight NGOs of the state by sanctioning Rs. 6.52 lakh for training of educated unemployed 400 rural youth entrepreneurs of Arunachal Pradesh during the past 4 years for setting up enterprises under self employment. NABARD has also provided support to 12 Skill Development Programme (SDPs) in association with seven NGOs of the state by sanctioning Rs. 4.14 lakh for imparting skills to 300 rural persons of Arunachal Pradesh to enable them to get wage employment or self employment. The Rural Haat scheme is to facilitate marketing of farm and non-firm produce of the farmers and entrepreneurs for which NABARD has sanctioned Rs. 3.0 lakh to a SHG in Injonu village of Lower Subansiri district for construction of Rural Haat. The marketing outlet will benefit cultivators of nearly four villages for selling their agro/horticulture produce. Under Tribal Development Fund (TDF) NABARD has sanctioned a project 'ASISI PAALU' to cover 500 families in six years in Roing, lower Dibang Valley district through Essomi Foundation with a total project outlet is Rs. 143.95 lakh. The fruit crops identified are orange and pineapple over 500 acres of land for 500 tribal families.

The SHG-Bank Linkage programme conceptualized and launched by NABARD in 1992 attempts to link the poor in large numbers to the formal banking sector in a sustainable and cost-effective manner. The objective is to increase the accessibility of financial services to a large number of rural people who are excluded from the banking system. As on 31st March 2008, 1312 SHGs were formed by Banks and NGOs out of which 651 SHGs were credit linked with banks in the state of Arunachal Pradesh. In recent year, 6 capacity building programmes have been conducted to 152 members of SHGs. NABARD has assisted two NGOs for formation of SHGs in the state. NABARD is providing technical and financial support for training and capacity-building and exposure visits of 80 master trainers, 2500 SHG promoters, standardization & supply of stationery to 5000 SHGs and developing MIS under Microfinance Vision 2011 of the State Government. During 2008-09 an amount of Rs. 15 lakh has been released as interest-free loan for setting up Dairy units to 10 beneficiaries under Venture Capital Fund for Dairy and Poultry Sectors in Arunachal Pradesh.

Role of State Commission for Women in promotion of SHG

The Arunachal Pradesh State Commission for Women, a statutory body set up with the purpose of protecting the interest of women and to ensure their progress and development, has adopted intensive advocacy for formation and sustenance of SHGs, since its establishment in January 17, 2005 under the Chairmanship of Smt. Jarjum Ete. Presently, Miss Komoli Mosang, Chairperson, has kept alive, the agenda of economic empowerment of women, through encouraging economically viable activities. The recommendations evolved from grassroots experiences are provision of facilities for better economic opportunities in rural areas, strengthening of women's organizations, better livelihood opportunities for women and women's participation in development planning. Activities were undertaken since inception for realizing economic self-reliance among women through the medium of likeminded groups. The organization has conducted a public hearing on 'Micro Credit for Self Help Groups' on 17th January 2006 and a two day state-level orientation workshop on 'SHGs-Resource Mobilization and Launching of the RMK' and public hearing on 'livelihood concerns of urban women with marginal income' on December 15, 2007.

Role of Social Welfare Department in promotion of SHG

Indira Mahila Yojana was redesigned as integrated programme for Women Empowerment and renamed as 'Swayam Siddha' under department of Social Welfare, Women and Child Development. The board mandates the programme for women empowerment (social and economic) with access to financial services and wider participation in development planning. Since the establishment and recasting of the programme in 2001-02, 304 SHGs have been formed in five blocks viz. Buragaon in West Kameng district, Roing in Lower Dibang Valley, Sagalee in Papum Pare district, Pangin in East Siang and Seppa in East Kameng district and are engaged in micro-credit and micro-enterprise development. Under Swayam Siddha the activities undertaken by the department are community mobilization, capacity-building of the group, saving and credit linkage of SHGs, creating a database, counseling and monitoring of the groups and networking amongst different stakeholders for effective and convergence of the programme. The department has extended help for formation of SHG Federation through clustering of SHGs. One such successful federation is the Sagalee Sub-division SHG Federation.

Case study-I

Although Arunachal has started late on Microfinance activities, but not lagging behind in creating success stories.

It is a success story of an SHG in Arunachal Pradesh, throwing light on how the SHG members were successful in changing their lives with the help of SHGs. The 'KHIJILI' is a SHG of women of Injonu village under Koronu circle of Lower Dibang Valley district of Arunachal Pradesh. The group was promoted and guided by 'GYANODYA' a renowned NGO in 2003 and had opened a bank account in Arunachal Pradesh State Co-operative Apex Bank with transactions of Rs. 2.00 lakh with their monthly savings. The group is having regular monthly collection. The internal lending of the group and repayment from the members is regular. The group has also successfully utilized the scheme sanctioned under SGSY for creating an asset. The group purchased a tractor, run successfully and repaid entire bank loan. Now the group is proud with the owner of a tractor which is used for hiring and transportation of agriculture produce. Impressed by the success story of the group, NABARD in association with Essomi Foundation Trust has sanctioned a grant assistance of Rs. 3.0 lakh to the SHG for construction of Rural Haat. The SHG has completed the construction and the Haat is being used by nearby villagers for sale of their produce.

Case study-II

It is a success story of SHGs at Lekang of Lohit district of Arunachal Pradesh. During 2006-07, 14 women SHGs with membership of 159 were provided training under Piggery (four groups) and Fisheries (10 groups). All these SHGs were provided finance by NABARD of Rs. 18.0 lakh. The group has started their production in January 2009. Under Piggery, they have produce 3670 kgs pork and 108 piglets out of which 3450 kgs. Pork and 108 piglets were sold. The groups have also sold the entire production of 49.5 quantities of fishery. All the SHGs are in profit and have stated repaying bank loan. This success of the SHGs has boosted up to initiate SHG movement in the circle which has led to formed 102 groups by various departments viz. Swayam Siddha scheme of Social Welfare department, ATMA, Nehru Yuva Kendra etc. out of which 90 per cent are women groups. These SHGs have taken up various income generating activities viz. vegetable cultivation, broiler farming, sericulture, etc. which has improved not only their income level but also brought social empowerment.

Constraints and challenges

Micro-credit is in its evolutionary process and requires a large number of reforms with regard to objectives and operations. A study of the working of Micro Credit in Latin America, Asia and Africa conducted by Women's World Banking and Monitor Company in 2004, has revealed certain inherent features of the system which have emerged over the years. These are:

- Microfinance clients want more, faster and better. They value speed and convenience; they want access to larger loans. They want respect and recognition and they care about interest rate.
- Low income men and women define microfinance broadly. They want business loans. They want to deposit voluntary savings. They want housing and education loans. They want health and life insurance. And they are willing to pay what it costs to provide responsive, sustainable services.
- Poor people prefer individual loans over group loans. As their experience grows, clients of group loans resent the time that group meetings take, and the need to guarantee repayment by other members of the group.
- The challenge in microfinance is not high risk but high transaction costs in making very small loans and in mobilizing small savings.
- Microfinance is not a mature industry. The leaders continue to innovate on products, processes and distribution systems to reduce time and costs.

- Microfinance performs well in good times and outperforms corporate finance in bad times. Poor women have demonstrated that they are the world's best borrowers.

There are some serious constraints with regard to expansion of microfinance portfolios. These exist in the form of :

- Interest rate ceilings;
- Insufficient commitment from govt. banks etc.
- Prevailing culture, which is biased against small transactions and poor borrowers;
- Inadequate knowledge of appropriate methodologies;
- Inappropriate human capital, particularly among loan officers.

There are however, some major exceptions to the above. Some banks and finance companies are seeking a future in small transactions because they recognize that the majority of the economically active people are low income entrepreneurs and producers.

Need for holistic approach

While the concept of Livelihood Finance calls for strengthening the microfinancing and providing some additional services which helps the microfinance to graduate to micro-enterprise financing. There will always be a need for micro-credit even if the element of livelihood finance is added to it. The theory of creating large and sustainable employment to large units is just one of the concepts. This is also into a substitute for micro-credit. In a growing country like India which faces the problem of large scale poverty and unemployment, there is a need for all the three, i.e., micro-credit, livelihood finance and job creation through large enterprises. In fact, an ideal situation is one in which there is proper integration among all the three.

Conclusion

The work is full of examples where poor women have succeeded in improving their life through membership in SHG. The impact on their lives is not just an economic one, gaining more self-confidence is often a more lasting achievement that forms the basis for social and economic improvements. Microfinance attempts to unleash forces transforming lives from debt-driven to self-driven, so as to cause and trigger growth in rural economics. The focus of microfinance is to facilitate the shift from induced development from the above to initiated development from below that is likely to change the role of bank credit in the rural segment. More than one-third of credit needs in the rural areas are still met by informal and high cost resources such as moneylenders, landlords, friends and relatives, and as such the scope for the microfinance to make inroads in rural segment is quite enormous. There are some vital issues that need to be addressed as below:

- Scaling up the SHG with both forward and backward linkages.
- Capacity-building and holistic approach to handle SHG.
- Setting up a supervisory body like National Centre for Excellence in Micro-Finance.
- Streamline legal framework to remove the infirmities, documentation, stamp duty, records and books of account, grading of SHGs.
- Ensure better co-ordination between the formal financial institutions and the informal ones such as MFIs.
- Encourage setting up of adequate Non-Governmental Organizations, Voluntary Agencies, etc.
- Sensitize the banking sector to view microfinance as a commercially viable business proposition so as to leverage their network.

- Formulate innovative schemes to finance micro-enterprise through the largest postal network in India as there is good penetration and hands-on approach available.

Above all, the mainstream financial institutions and microfinancial institutions are required to play an increasingly important and prominent role in nourishing and developing microfinance sector as social obligation. Credit needs of the poor are increasingly met from the emergence of a wide range of semi-formal microfinance initiatives. Considering various advantages, particularly the financing of the rural poor, low transactional cost and better recovery performance, the banks have a great role to play in the microfinance sector. Unless the poor have access to financial services to meet their needs for consumption and productive activities for meeting emergencies, any development assistance would not be sustainable.

REFERENCES

1. Approach Paper to Eleventh Five Year plan, Planning Commission, New Delhi.
2. Arunachalam, R. (1999), *Alternative Technologies in the Indian Micro-Finance Industry*, New Delhi, Action Aid.
3. Arun, *Self Help*, Volume 1, Issue 1, 2009, pp. 1-4.
4. Das Gupta, R. (2005), "Microfinance in India", *EPW*, March. New Delhi.
5. Das Gupta, R. (2006), "An Architectural Plan for Microfinance Institutional Network," *Economic and Political Weekly*, New Delhi.
6. Microfinance Vision 2011, Govt. of Arunachal Pradesh, December 29, 2008, pp. 1-7.
7. Priya B. and Srivastav P. (2005), "Exploring possibilities—Microfinance and Rural Credit Access for the Poor in India," *Economic and Political Weekly*.
8. Rangarajan C. (2005), High Level Policy Conference on Microfinance in India, New Delhi.
9. RBI's Working Group (1995), *Non-Governmental Organizations and Self-Help Group*, NABARD.

10. Raghavan R. S. (2006), *Microfinance—Uplifting of Rural Economy*, the Chartered Accountant, p. 1145.
11. Satyamurti, V. and Haokip, S. (2002) *Microfinance: Concepts and Delivery Channels in India*, New Delhi, AIAMED.
12. http://www.alternative-finance.org.uk/cgibin/summary.pl?id=151&language=E
13. SIDBI Reading Material, Lucknow.
14. Wilson, K. (2002), "The Role of Self Help Group Bank Linkage Programme in preventing rural emergencies in India." NABARD Seminar on SHG-bank Linkage Programme, New Delhi, November, 2002.
15. World Bank-Asia Technical Development Report 1995.
16. http://www.indiaprofile.com
17. http://www.indiamart.com
18. http://www.virtualbangalore.com
19. http://www.indiantravelportal.com/maps-of-india
20. http://www.upportal.com/infrastructure/g_noida.asp
21. http://www.techno-preneur.net
22. http:/www.smallindustryindia.com
23. http://www.nabard.org/roles/mcid/shgbanklink.htm
24. http://www.newdelhi.mfa.no/Development+Cooperation/Default.htm#Women

6

An Evaluation of Microfinance Scheme in Andhra Pradesh

A Study of Selected Members of the SHGs in Guntur District

*Dr. G.V. Chalam

Introduction

Now a days, poverty eradication has been the primary concern of every state, but these poverty alleviation efforts through state driven credit supply schemes produced only sub-optimal results. In order to get effective use of these programmes, effective arrangements shall be made for delivery and effective use of credit to the rural poor. The failure of the formal credit institutions in meeting the credit requirements of rural poor has been the major reason for innovations in microfinance. The most complex problem in rural credit delivery system is serving small loans and making available the credit to the unreached and uncared so far, that too an adequate amount at the right time with minimum documentation requirements.

In this direction, a non-formal agency for credit supply to the poor, in the name of Self Help Group (SHG) Scheme

* M.Com., LL.M., M.B.A., Ph.D., Department of Commerce and Business Administration, Acharya Nagarjuna University, Nagarjuna Nagar-522 510, A.P.

could emerge as a promising partner to the formal credit system, which is based on the philosophy of organizing the poorest of the poor and make them realized the very basic mission of 'theory of survival'. This concept has been praised worldwide in a 'Micro Credit Summit' that was organized in 1997 and a decision was taken to extend credit for self-employment activities. Thus, the SHGs formed as instruments for the socio-economic development of the rural people. Of late, they are participating in several developmental programmes of the state, beyond the thrift and credit activities.

More specifically, the following are the objectives of the Self Help Group Scheme:

- To inculcate the savings and banking habits among the SHGs members.
- To secure them with financial, technical and moral strengths.
- To enable the group to avail loan for productive purposes and repaying the same over a period of time and in the process to gain economic prosperity.
- To obtain the collective wisdom in organizing and managing their own funds and distributing the benefits among themselves.

The SHG-Bank Linkage Programme launched by NABARD in 1992 is a landmark in the field of microfinancing in India. This Programme aims to organize SHGs of 10 to 20 persons from the economically homogenous group to attain the above said common objectives of the SHGs. These SHGs consist of members who are economically poor, having low saving capacity and who depend on moneylenders or other private sources for meeting their basic needs and other productive purposes. In other words, a typical SHG will consist of like-minded individuals who can regularly save small amounts of money.

To facilitate group process and ensure transparency of operations, group meetings are regularly convened at a pre-determined date, place and time. The thrift amounts are pooled and given out as loan to SHG members for productive or investment purposes based on the priorities decided by the group. Since, it is members' thrift that is given out as loan to one or two members each time depending upon the priorities set by the group and the members' utilization of this loan. Similarly, peer or moral pressure is exerted on members to continue savings to enable every member an opportunity to avail loans. Likewise, the left out members also insists prompt repayment of loan in anxiety to avail loan of higher order. As a result, at any given point of time all members in the Self-Help Group are not borrowers and even if all of them are borrowers, their loan amount outstanding will not be equal.

Need of the study

The studies conducted by the NABARD, commercial banks, policy-makers and economic thinkers have proved that financing of SHGs has contributed significantly in reduction of transaction costs, besides reducing the financial risk and increasing the recovery performance. Further, the SHGs are fast emerging agencies for the socio-economic development of the rural people. The government is also very keen on raising the standards of living of this rural mass through various developmental schemes.

Therefore, the present study is an attempt to evaluate the working of SHGs and their impact on the socio-economic conditions of the members of the SHGs. The studies of this type may be useful in taking corrective measures in the existing practices and point out what more to be attended for the effective working of these schemes. No attempt has been made so far in this direction to study the working performance of the SHGs, which would help the funding agencies, policy-makers, and government. The working performance of the SHGs and their impact on the socio-economic conditions of the members can be studied by conducting a survey on the opinions of the members of these schemes. Keeping in view of this aim, the following are the specific objectives of the present study.

Objectives of the study

(*i*) To study the impact of the SHG scheme on the socio-economic conditions of the members in the selected area of the study.

(*ii*) To analyze the SHG members' perceptions about the SHG scheme and identify the reasons for the success of the SHG concept;

(*iii*) To offer suggestions for the effective working of SHG scheme for the attainment of its objectives.

Methodology of the study

The study is confined to examine the impact of SHG scheme on the socio-economic conditions of its members by invoking their opinions on the SHG concept and to evaluate the performance of these SHGs. The other aspects like administrative policies, designing of schemes, etc. arc excluded from the purview of the present study. For the evaluation of the SHG concept and its impact, there is a need to select the SHGs and their members. Due to time and resources constraints, the desirability of choosing a logically more convenient area predisposed the researcher towards selecting his own native district, i.e. Guntur in A.P.

At the latter stage, a village was selected which is more accessible for the collection of data on the perception of members about the scheme and its impact. For this, Vejendla village is selected which is a sizeable village having a nationalized bank caters to the banking needs of the members of the SHGs. Moreover, there were no empirical studies conducted so far in this part of the district. Since this study is intended to elicit the opinions of the members of the

SHGs on their working and usefulness, it is proposed to interview the members with a structured schedule. For this, the SHGs members are selected at random from different SHGs working in the selected area of the study. Further, to study the impact of SHG scheme, a period of three years is selected. In fact, a study of this type normally requires at least a 5-year period, and hence, the recent five years period is chosen ranging from 2003-04 to 2007-08.

The data for the analysis is collected both from primary and secondary sources. Since, the data on the perceptions of the members needed is primary in nature the survey method is adopted. Besides, the data is also collected, wherever necessary from the records of the bank that finances the SHGs, IBA bulletins, magazines and circulars issued by the Reserve Bank of India and NABARD from time to time on the working of SHGs.

ANALYSIS OF THE STUDY

In this section, the analysis is made to elicit the opinions of the members of Self-Help Groups on the concept and its impact on the socio-economic conditions of the members. For this, the members were asked the information with the help of a structured questionnaire and collected the relevant data for the analysis.

Socio-cultural impact of Self-Help Group scheme

Although various rural development programmes for the benefit of the weaker sections are available, the present SHG scheme is very much useful for the eradication of poverty. It is expected to bring about an improvement in the socio-cultural conditions in a more effective manner. In the light of this, the present section aims at analyzing the social contacts with the economic aspects of developmental programmes. For this purpose, the data are analyzed with respect to:

(*i*) Changes in Socio-cultural habits.

(*ii*) Mobility and media exposure.

(*iii*) Public contacts with officials/non-officials.

(*iv*) Social, cultural and political participation.

Changes in socio-cultural habits

Even though it was found in various studies that the socio-cultural habits of the members, such as type of food, cultural habits, children education, awareness of development programmes, etc. here the aim is to find out whether the post-SHG membership period has any edge over the pre-SHG membership period by virtue of his becoming member and additional incomes flows from the scheme or by his additional man-days of employment.

The data with regard to the various socio-cultural habits of the SHG members are collected for both the periods and are presented in Table 6.1. The habits taken for the analysis are: consumption of hygienic food, changes in socio-cultural habits, schooling of children, and awareness of social developmental programmes.

Table 6.1 : Adoption of different socio-cultural practices of SHG members during the pre- and post-membership periods

Type of Practice	Pre-SHG period	Post-SHG period	% of Change
1. Use of hygienic food	21/35 (60.0)	26/35 (74.2)	5/35 (14.3)
2. Awareness of developmental programs	21/35 (60.0)	26/35 (74.2)	5/35 (14.3)
3. Socio-cultural habits	8/35 (22.8)	18/35 (51.4)	10/35 (28.5)
4. Schooling of children	36/96 (37.5)	44/96 (45.8)	8/96 (8.3)

Note : 1. Sample size is adjusted to the applicable cases.
2. Figures in parentheses are percentages.

Source: Compiled from the collected data.

The table 6.1 shows that there are about 30 per cent of the SHG members improved in social, cultural habits during the post-SHG membership period by involving in social, cultural programmes. The responses relating to the members of the SHG scheme are analyzed in this regard. A clear and positive change can be obtained with respect to the food habits, involvement of social development programmes and also educating children during the post-SHG membership period, which may partly be due to the additional awareness in the latter period.

Mobility and media exposure

Mobility enables a person not only to observe things outside his own community-belt, but also to come into contact with people who have different habits, attitudes, values and practices. The experience of exposing oneself to a wide area of human activity and interaction with people other than those who are known intimately leads to widening of horizons and an increase in knowledge. The cumulative effect of increased mobility gives a general feeling of self-confidence. With this background, it is designed to measure the degree of mobility and to know how far the SHG members have increased their mobility before and after SHG membership.

Mobility

In the present study, the mobility of respondents is measured in terms of the frequency of their mobility, visits to the outside villages and the nearest town. The information is collected and classified as low, medium and high mobility basing on the average number of visits.

Table 6.2 presents the data on the mobility of the SHG members during pre- and post-membership periods. The data are arranged across three levels of mobility classes. It can be seen from the data that the degree of mobility is increased from low to medium and higher mobility classes have shown a positive change of about 16.0 per cent during the period of study. This increased mobility may be partly because of procedural visits required by the bankers and other officials connected with the DRDA schemes.

Table 6.2: Mobility of the SHG members during the pre- and post-SHG membership periods

Degree of Mobility	Pre-SHG period	Post-SHG period	% of Change
Low (0-3)	42 (38.8)	31 (28.8)	– 9 (21.4)
Medium (3-6)	36 (33.3)	42 (38.8)	6 (16.6)
High (6-9)	30 (27.9)	35 (32.4)	5 (16.6)
Total	**108 (100.0)**	**108 (100.0)**	—

Note: Figures in parentheses are percentages.
Source: Compiled from the collected data.

Media exposure

Media exposure in the form of information on agricultural and allied activities, propaganda and entertainment are institutionalized. The relatively low cost of mass media especially radio as a means of disseminating information has enabled its use by developmental agencies. The radio, and more recently television are considered important mass media. Interviews with agricultural and other experts, demonstration of new occupational practices on television, recreational home-forum and others have been known to be of high interest value. Newspapers and magazines have since long been recognized as means of information in respect of local and distant news.

An attempt is, therefore, made to measure the extent of exposure of the SHG members towards newspapers, radio and television. The data collected are scored and classified into low, medium and high levels of media exposure and presented in Table 6.3.

Table 6.3: Media exposure of SHG members during the pre- and post-membership periods

Degree of Exposure	Pre-SHG period	Post-SHG period	% of Change
Low (0-3)	84 (77.8)	56 (51.8)	-38 (45.3)
Medium (3-6)	12 (11.1)	39 (36.2)	+27 (225.0)
High (6-9)	12 (11.1)	13 (12.0)	+1 (8.3)
Total	**108 (100.0)**	**108 (100.0)**	—

Note: Figure in parentheses are percentages.
Source: Compiled from the collected data.

Table 6.3 shows that about 77.8 per cent of the respondents are exposed to very low degree of media exposure during the pre-SHG period, but the position is changed in the later period. Now, as many as 50.0 per cent of the respondents are in the medium and higher degree media exposure may be because of the relative change with respect to the visits frequently to the nearest towns.

Public contacts with officials and non-officials

The officials and non-officials are called the 'change agents' who are placed at various levels in the district administration including the 'block' and 'village'. At the village level, the Panchayats are the basic units of self-government, who serve as important instruments for enlisting people's participation as well as implementation of developmental activities. Next to panchayats, block level administration serves as an important unit, which has made the services of the government more accessible to the people and also enabled to build a closer and continuous interaction between the people and the government.

The respondents' awareness and contacts with officials are studied in respect of officials like the Block Development Officer, Extension Officer, District Agricultural Officer, Veterinary Officer, Village Development Officer and P.H.C doctor. The non-officials include village sarpanch, presidents of co-operative societies, MLAs, MPs, etc.

Table 6.4: SHG members' contacts with official/non-officials during pre- and post-SHG membership periods

Degree of Contacts	Pre-SHG period	Post-SHG period	% of Change
Low (0-5)	77 (71.2)	19 (17.5)	–58 (75.3)
Medium (5-10)	22 (20.3)	73 (67.5)	51 (231.8)
High (10-15)	09 (8.3)	16 (14.8)	07 (77.7)
Total	**108 (100.0)**	**108 (100.0)**	—

Note: Figures in parentheses are percentages.
Source: Compiled from the collected data

The responses are presented in Table 6.4 in respect of members' awareness and contacts with both the officials and non-officials during the period of study. The data on members' contacts with official/non-officials explain that there is a substantial change with respect to these contacts during the post-SHG period. While about 71.2 per cent of the respondents are with lower contacts during pre-SHG period and now about 81.0 per cent of them are at higher-level contacts. This position may be due to their contacts with bank officers, politicians, etc., to get loan sanctioned under the SHG scheme.

Social participation

The past decade witnessed a rise in the importance of grass-root organization and the extent to which people liked activities. The social participation, thus, runs through the entire spectrum of economic and social development. The individual participation in formal and non-formal organizations enables a person to have direct access to a number of inputs and information. If an individual is become a member of various organizations, i.e., social, cultural, religious and political, more benefits are likely to accrue to him.

Participation is taken as a variable and is measured in terms of participation in meetings of elected village pacnchayats, co-operative societies, school committees, and the cultural participation including dramas, games and sports. The religious participation includes associating with temple committees and political participation, including voting in panchayats, assembly and parliament elections.

Table 6.5: Social participation of members of SHG during pre- and post-SHG membership periods

(Multiple reasons)

	Pre-SHG period	Post-SHG period	% of Change
Village panchayat meetings	6 (5.5)	8 (7.4)	+ 2 (33.3)
Cooperative societies meetings	2 (1.8)	4 (3.7)	+ 2 (100.0)
School committee meetings	—	1 (0.9)	+ 1 (100.0)
Caste panchayat	26 (24.0)	38 (35.1)	+ 12 (46.1)
Dramas, sports and games	18 (16.6)	20 (18.4)	+ 2 (11.1)
Assembly and parliament elections	101 (93.5)	108 (100.0)	+ 7 (6.9)
	108	**108**	—

The data presented in Table 6.5, indicate that expecting the participation in elections, very poor social participation is associated with the respondents during the pre-SHG period. It may be due to the fact that the borrowers are economically weak during the pre-SHG period. This position is not substantially changed even during the post-SHG period.

Hence, it can be concluded that the participation in social activities is not only influenced by the economic status but also of other factors like education, family background, caste, etc.

Table 6.6 presents the data on the participation of SHG members in various social developmental programmes.

Table 6.6: Participation of Self-Help Group members in various social development programmes

Type of Programme	Number of members	% in Total
Social awareness activities	34	31.5
Janmabhoomi programme	28	25.9
Health and family welfare programmes	22	20.4
Promotion of thrift/savings	16	14.8
Promotion of education/vocational skills	08	07.4
Total	**108**	**100.0**

Source: Compiled from the collected data.

It can be observed from the data in Table 6.6 that among the various identified social developmental programmes, more number of members involved in the social awareness activities (31.5) which are organized to remove the social evils and traditions, that work against perpetuation of social and gender inequality such as casteism, untouchables, child marriages, etc. Next to it, Janmabhomi programme (25.9) is an innovative programme, which is a mechanism for the mobilization and involvement of the people in community development activities in general and women development programmes in particular. Health and family welfare programmes (20.4) are also one of the important social activities taken-up by the SHG members to create the health awareness among the people who are living in slum areas. In this programme a special attention is paid towards the pregnancy of women who should take special health care and to take good food. Though they are not very significant, other activities undertaken by the SHGs are to promote thrift/ savings (14.8) among members of the group and develop the education and vocational skills (7.4).

Table 6.7: Different reasons expressed by the respondents to join as Self-Help Group members

Different Reason	Number of members	% in Total
Savings	49	45.5
Self-help	38	35.5
Availing of loans	16	14.5
Encourage by others	03	02.5
Other causes	02	02.0
Total	**108**	**100.0**

Source: Compiled from the collected data.

Table 6.7 shows the data on the reasons of membership in SHGs. It can be seen from the data that among the various reasons identified for joining SHGs; majority (45.5) of the respondents expressed that savings as the main purpose followed by self-help (35.5), and opportunities for availing loans (14.5). The other reasons, like force or encouragement by others are not playing much role in admitting the members in these groups. It can be concluded from the foregoing discussion that the main reason to join people in the SHGs is to save amount out of their earnings, which is also the objective of microfinance concept.

Economic impact of SHG scheme

This section aims at the following in evaluating the impact of the SHG scheme on the structural pattern of employment, generation of income and additional assets of the sample members of the study. More specifically, and also to understand the various problems faced by the SHG members in this context. The economic development of any society is the result of deliberate, conscious and planned efforts of the government towards the nation goals. To improve the quality of life of a large majority of population, a plan has to encompass automatically the economic and social goals along with a scheme for the development of physical, economic and social infrastructure as well as building-up of capabilities of the target-groups to make the best use of the infrastructure made available.

Following the introduction of the various developmental schemes, there has been a rise in output resulting in higher incomes and acquisition of capital assets as well as durable consumer goods, especially by the beneficiaries. This is to be reflected in the levels of living and the change in economic status, having effect on social aspects of development as well.

Now, an attempt is made in this section to analyze the economic aspects of the sample members during the period with respect to the following aspects:

(*i*) Employment generation;

(*ii*) Asset accruals;

(*iii*) Changes in annual income;

(*iv*) Savings.

Employment generation

A change in the number of days of gainful employment to one's own vocation provides a measure of shift in the economic condition of one's family. In the present paper the SHG scheme has shown the impact on the employment pattern and on the number of days of employment of the members' families. A positive impact in this regard is highly desirable. Hence, it is proposed to study the impact of the SHG scheme in creating additional man-days of employment to the members' family.

Table 6.8: Distribution of members on the basis of man-days of employment per member during the pre- and post-SHG membership periods

Number of employment man-days per family in a year	Number of members			
	Pre-SHG membership period		Post-SHG membership period	
	No. of members	%	No. of members	%
Up to 60	8	8	—	08
60 – 120	26	27	4	22
120 – 180	32	31	22	10
180 – 240	23	23	36	13
240 – 300	10	10	24	14
above 300	09	09	22	13
Total	**108**	**100**	**108**	**100**

Table 6.8 shows the distribution of the SHG member families as against different classes of man-days of employment during the pre-SHG scheme and post-SHG scheme periods. The data presented are based on seven categories of man-days of family employment. A substantial position, i.e., about 73.0 per cent of the members of SHGs is found in the first four categories of employment during the pre-SHG scheme period. Two groups covering more than 50.0 per cent of the families are found in the employment group of 120 to 360 days during the pre-SHG scheme period and thus an average, a member's family is found engaged in a different vocation for 313 days in a year during this period. Whereas, the member of man-days of employment increased from 318 to 414 days due to the support of SHGs

during the post-SHG scheme period. Now, more than 50.0 per cent of the members are now in the range of 240 to 600 man-days of employment after admitting the SHG scheme. It can be concluded from the foregoing analysis that the SHG scheme has enabled the member families to improve by an additional average of 100 man-days of family employment. However, this increase is found to be not a substantial one as the computed F-value is not significant at 5.0 per cent level.

Asset accruals

The changes in assets are natural to the beneficiaries of any developmental scheme. As different scheme assets are being distributed through the SHG scheme, the member family gets an additional asset base to improve the income of the

Table 6.9: Distribution of members according to asset accruals during pre- and post-SHG membership periods

Asset Value	Number of members		Change in number	% of Change
	Pre-SHG period	Post-SHG period		
Below 10,000	39 (36.11)	31 (28.70)	8	20.5
10,001 – 25,000	26 (26.85)	19 (17.59)	7	26.9
25,001 – 50,000	16 (14.81)	14 (12.96)	2	12.5
50,001 – 1,00,000	13 (12.03)	18 (16.66)	5	38.5
1, 00,001 – 5,00,000	6 (5.55)	13 7 (12.04)	116.7	—
Above 75,00,000	8 (7.14)	13 (12.04)	5	62.5
	108 (100.0)	**108 (100.0)**	—	—

family. Further these additional assets may also accrue to family if the point of re-investment of generated income is considered. Now, an attempt is made to analyze the changes in the asset-pattern of the members of the SHGs.

Table 6.9 presents the distribution of members of SHGs across the different groups of assets and the data are presented among seven categories ranging from zero to Rs. 20,000. About 78.0 per cent of the members are found in the first three groups of assets with an asset value of Rs. 4,000. It can be observed from the data presented in the table, that there is a positive change in the asset pattern of SHG members. The average asset value of these members during the pre-SHG scheme period is Rs. 3,421.30. It is also evident that there is a positive change in the accruals of assets holdings and it has increased from Rs. 3,421.30 to Rs. 5,592.59. The increases in asset holding are found good in the first four categories of asset classes and it enabled them to cross over the limits of those classes. The variations in the member of members falling in each asset group are less during the post-SHG scheme period (112.43) when compared to the pre-SHG scheme period (166.43). This lowering variation enables one to conclude that the assets given under the SHG scheme enabled the lower classes of population to strengthen the asset base. It reduces naturally the gap between haves and have-nots with respect to the distribution of assets among the members.

The foregoing analysis enables to conclude that the loans to SHG scheme have enabled the respondents to improve their assets with an average amount of more than Rs. 11,000 during the period of study. However, this accrual of assets is not found substantial, as the computed F-value is not significant at 0.05 per cent level.

Changes in Annual Income

It is quite obvious that a change in additional investment leads to a change in the annual income. Notably the generation of additional man-days of employment and accrual of additional assets automatically raise the annual income of any individual. In the present analysis, it is proposed to study the impact of SHG scheme on the annual income of the members during the period of study.

Table 6.10 : Distribution of members according to annual family income size during pre- and post-SHG membership period

Annual income (Amount in Rs.)	Number of members		Change in number	% of Change
	Pre-SHG period	Post-SHG period		
< 10,000	16 (14.8)	7 (6.5)	9	56.3
10001 - 20000	26 (24.7)	17 (15.9)	9	34.5
20001 – 30000	27 (25.0)	23 (21.2)	4	14.8
30001 – 40000	19 (19.6)	28 (25.9)	9	47.4
40001 – 50000	15 (13.9)	26 (24.1)	11	73.4
> 50000	5 (4.6)	7 (6.5)	2	40.0
	108 (100.0)	**108 (100.0)**	—	—

Table 6.10 depicts the distribution of SHG members according to the annual income during pre- and post-SHG membership periods. The data are arranged among six categories of income groups ranging between zero and Rs.10,000. It is observed from the data presented in the table that a remarkable percentage (64.5) per cent of members are found in the first three groups with a maximum amount of Rs. 5,000. It shows that about 66.7 per cent of the borrowers live with substance level of income during pre-

SHG membership period. On an average, each member earns an amount of Rs. 4,391.20 per annum during pre-SHG membership period. It can also be identified from the data that a noticeable improvement is found in the annual income of the members during the post-SHG membership period. The borrowers of lower income categories have moved to the higher classes of annual income. After availing themselves of the loan facility from the sponsoring bank under this scheme, 50.0 per cent of the members are able to get an annual income of more than Rs. 5,000. It implies that a considerable amount of positive change is achieved in the incremental income of these members. The average annual income increased from Rs. 4,391.20 to Rs. 5,635.30 per SHG member family. This has enabled many to cross the poverty line. This favorable impact is found substantial as the computed F-value (10.14) is also found significant at 0.05 levels. It is also identified that the variations in the annual incomes of the respondents are very less during the post-SHG scheme period when compared to the pre-SHG membership period. It may be due to the relative stability in income-earning sources during the post-SHG membership period. Thus, it can be inferred from the foregoing analysis that there is a good amount of impact on the generation of income to the members by the SHG scheme during the post-SHG membership period.

Savings

Savings are the residue of income over expenses. It is very common to an individual to retain something out of his earnings. Like-wise every member out of his generated income saves something and uses it either for expansion or for developmental purposes. In the present analysis, it is planned to portray the savings pattern of SHG members in the selected sample during the study period.

Table 6.11: Distribution of members according to savings during pre- and post-SHG membership periods

Saving per your (Amount in Rs.)	Number of members		Change in number	% of Change
	Pre-SHG period	Post-SHG period		
Nil	16 (14.8)	5 (4.6)	11	68.75
< 1000	17 (15.7)	15 (13.9)	2	11.76
1001–2000	59 (54.6)	64 (59.3)	5	8.47
2001–3000	10 (9.3)	16 (14.8)	6	60.00
> 3000	06	08	2	33.33
	108	108	26	
X	**1296**	**1551**		

Table 6.11 presents the information on the distribution of the members' savings ranging from Rs. zero to Rs. 1,000 in five categories under SHG scheme. It is pertinent to note that more than 54.0 per cent of the member respondents are able to save only about Rs. 200 to 500 per annum during the pre-SHG membership period. An about 15.0 per cent of the members are not able to save anything. On an average, the members are able to save Rs. 345.83 out of their average annual income of Rs. 4,391.20 per family, which works out to only about 7.87 per cent of the gross income earned by them. The SHG scheme is able to improve the situation, through not substantially, of about 24.0 per cent of the members.

Thus, it can be concluded from the foregoing discussions that there is a positive impact of the credit under the SHG scheme on the generation of man-days of employment, creation of additional assets and generation of additional annual income to the SHG member family. But members of the SHGs are not able to derive substantial benefit because of poor yields from the given scheme assets and diversion of a part of the amount of loan for other purposes.

Findings

Impact of SHG scheme on the social conditions of the members

- The group members have really internalized the concept of self-help and mutual help by supporting its members in social sectors too.
- The members are participating in socio-economic development programmes like literacy, health, nutrition, housing, primary education, sanitation, etc.
- By involving in the group activity leadership qualities are developed, they are free to meet any bank official without any fear and shyness and also decision-making skills are improved.
- Providing access to government programmes and services and thereby improved the social status.
- Promoting women participation in community governance and also helps in improvement of women empowerment.
- In some villages, prohibition of liquor is achieved with the intervention of SHG members.

Impact of SHG scheme on the economic conditions of the members

- The self-help group concept helped in improving the economic status of the members by forming a group to avail the credit made easily and thereby standards of living improved.
- They are developing self-employment activities and thereby improved their economic position.
- SHGs inculcate thrift habits and increase the level of savings among the members.

- The members are helping banks in recovery of overdue loans, and receiving respect and attention from banks.
- Desired shift in loaning pattern of the members from consumption to productive activities.
- Groups should be free to fix the rate of interest on all loans advanced from the common fund.

Conclusion

The findings of the study revealed several positive features which require a battery of imaginative themes and techniques for motivating society for common good. These include:

SHGs inculcate the saving habits and increase the productive capacities among rural poor and thus the earnings of the members shifted from consumption to productive activities. Improvement in loaning amounts of SHGs through internal capitalization. Participation in socio-economic development programmes like literacy, health, housing, sanitation, etc. by matured SHGs has contributed to overall empowerment of rural poor.

The following are the deficiencies of the scheme noticed which require exercise of vigilance:

- Loans to members only on entitlement basis without any reference to the purpose of the loan;
- Absence of proper and up-to-date record keeping and absence of rotation of leadership position among SHG members and irregular group meetings.
- Lack of proper understanding of SHGs among banks and governmental agencies and this leads to lack of confidence among the bank branches to extend loans to SHGs in the absence of NGOs.
- Insistence by the bank branches for blocking entire cash savings of SHGs with them and also collateral security for extending loans to SHGs.

Most of the above-mentioned problems reinforce the need for attitudinal change and functional orientation of field level functionaries of all agencies involved in the promotion and development of Self Help Groups.

Suggestions for the effective working of SHGs

The following areas are to be properly analyzed and strictly implemented in order to attain the objectives of the SHGs.

- The term of office bearers of the SHGs should be fixed, with a maximum period of one year. Longer terms allow consolidation of power, which weakens group cohesion and ability to decide and act effectively.
- It is necessary to impose restrictions for deviant behavior of the members. (for example, failure to repay the installments, arriving late for the meetings, chitchats during the course of meetings, smoking at meetings, etc.)
- Groups that meet every week tend to be better than those groups, which meet fortnightly or monthly. Hence, weekly meetings are largely preferred with a fixed day and time for SHGs to convene. Any changes could be made only under special circumstances and after adequate intimation to all members of the group.
- A good SHG should maintain the attendance register and minutes book for meetings, savings ledger; members pass book, receipt and payment vouchers, cash book and loan ledger. Attendance of all members is compulsory and a register should be maintained to that effect. Groups with average attendance i.e. below 75 per cent were considered to be weak.
- The term of office bearers should be fixed, with a maximum period of one year, longer terms allowed consolidation of power, which weakens the group cohesion and ability to decide and act effectively.
- Status symbols like the name of "President" should be avoided, as they tend to invest people with extra

authority and power; the term "representative" was found to be more appropriate for the office bearers.

- A saving by each SHG member is an indication of his/her commitment to the group and for personal growth and progress. Every member should be encouraged to save some amount each week from the beginning. A savings register should be maintained to that effect.
- Reduction in loan transaction cost for banks and borrower alike and simplified loaning procedure and documentation.
- SHGs help banks to expand good clientele base among rural poor.
- SHGs provide enabling environment for conscious leadership development, decentralized decision-making, peer pressure and sustainability of group action.
- If the common fund is treated as a mere channel of funds, the groups tend to be weak. The groups should therefore, be free to fix the rate of interest on all loans advanced from the common fund. If the common fund revolves briskly, it indicates that the group is "GOOD" large unutilized deposits in the banks indicated a "WEAK" group.
- Every SHG should be encouraged to participate and to take active role in the social programmes like, family planning, literacy rate improvement, and other similar activities which are beneficial to the village community.

REFERENCES

1. Economic Survey Report, 2004-05, 2005-06, Ministry of Finance, GOI, New Delhi.
2. Harper, M. (1998), "Why are commercial banks not entering the microfinance market?" Paper produced as consultant to SDC, October 1998.

3. Information Brochure, NABARD, Itanagar, Arunachal Pradesh, 2009, pp. 1-6.
4. Information Brochure, Arunachal Commission for Women, Itanagar, 2009, pp. 1-7.
5. Mohammad Y. (2004), *Expanding Micro Credit outreach to reach the Millennium Development Goals—Some issues for attention-attacking poverty with Micro Credit*, Ed. Ahmed and Hakim, University Press, Dhaka.
6. Mahajan,V. (2005), "From Micro Credit to Livelihood Finance," *Economic and Political Weekly.*
7. Mohammad Y. (2006), *Grameen Bank, Micro Credit and Millennium Development Goals,* Micro, Small and Medium Enterprises Development Act 2006, GOI, New Delhi Mid Term Appraisal of Tenth Five year Plan, Planning Commission, New Delhi.

7

Microfinance—Women Empowerment through Pavala Vaddi Strategy and other Government Schemes

A Study with Reference to Chittoor District, Andhra Pradesh

*K.S.S. Hari Prasad

ABSTRACT

Women empowerment has gained considerable significance in the recent past. Microfinance could be a solution to help them to extend their horizon and offer social recognition and empowerment. Microfinance brings the power of credit to the grassroots by way of loans to the poor without requirement of collateral or previous credit record. In India, microfinance scene is dominated by Self-Help Groups (SHGs). Bank Linkage Programme as a cost-effective mechanism for providing financial services to the unreached poor which has been successful not only in meeting financial needs of the rural poor women but also strengthen collective self-help capacities of the poor, leading to their empowerment. Empowerment programmes introduced by the Government like Pavala Vaddi scheme and other programmes like Insurance, Procurement, Marketing of Non-Timber Forest Produce (NTFP) and cattle

* M.Com., MFM, MFT, M.Phil., Research Scholar in Ph.D., College of Commerce, Management and Information Studies, Sri Venkateswara University, Tirupati.

improvement etc., under Indira Kranthi Patham are succeeded up to some extent. Some success stories of women in SHGs of Chittoor district, the area of study, are highlighted. In spite of the impressive figures, microfinance in Chittoor district (A.P) presently doing well but it should still put some efforts to create a massive impact in poverty alleviation, but if pursued with skill and opportunity, development of the poor, it holds the promise to alter the socio-economic face of the poor.

Introduction

From the time immemorial, it has been victimized that women have been marginalized in every economy. A high percentage of women are amongst the poorest of the poor. Women have been the vulnerable section of society and constitute a sizeable segment of the poverty struck population. Women face gender specific barriers to access education, health, employment etc. To alleviate the situation, Government has taken up the theme of women's empowerment as one of the strategies to tackle the socio-economic poverty. Since women's empowerment is the key to socio-economic development of the community, bringing women into the mainstream of national development has been a major concern of Government. Microfinance activities can give them a means to climb out of poverty. Microfinance could be a solution to help them to extend their horizon and offer social recognition and empowerment. Microfinance brings the power of credit to the grassroots by way of loans to the poor without requirement of collateral or previous credit record. Experience shows that microfinance can help the poor to increase income, build viable businesses, and reduce their vulnerability to external shocks. It can also be a powerful instrument of self-empowerment by enabling the poor, especially women, to become economic agents of change. It is understood that microfinance is workable and sustainable anywhere, where there is poverty. In India, microfinance scene is dominated by Self-Help Groups (SHGs)–Bank Linkage Programme as a cost-effective mechanism for providing financial services to the unreached poor which has been successful not only in meeting financial needs of the rural poor women but also strengthen collective self-help capacities of the poor, leading to their empowerment. Rapid progress in SHG formation has now turned into an empowerment movement among women across the country. Microfinance is necessary to overcome exploitation, create confidence for economic self-reliance of the rural poor particularly among rural women who are most invisible in the social structure.

Objectives of the study

The broad objective of the study is to examine the role and performance of SHGs and implementation of government schemes for the women empowerment in the study area. However, the study has some specific objectives. They are:

- To analyse the economic gains derived by the members after joining the SHGs.
- To examine the social benefits derived by the members after joining in the groups.
- To analyse the operating system of SHGs for the mobilization of saving, delivery of credit to the needy, management of group funds, repayment of loans, in building up leadership, and establishing linkage with banks
- To analyze the SHGs in the study area, the impact of implementation of government schemes.

Selection of study area and sample units

The study was carried out in selective clusters and certain mandals of Chittoor district in Andhra Pradesh.

Data collected from the Mandal Development Offices, and by personal meetings with SHGs and individuals. Gone through various reports and books.

Review of literature

The concept of empowerment is defined as the process by which women take control and ownership of their choices. The core elements of empowerment have been defined as agency (the ability to define one's goals and act upon them), awareness of gendered power structures, self-esteem, and self-confidence (Kabeer, 2001). Empowerment can take place at a hierarchy of different levels—individual, household, community and societal—and is facilitated by providing encouraging factors (e.g. exposure to new activities, which can build capacities) and removing inhibiting factors (e.g. lack of resources and skills). In this connection, Microfinance with Self-Help Groups play an effective role for promoting women empowerment. It is not only an efficient tool to fight against poverty, but also as a means of promoting the empowerment of the most marginalized sections of the population, especially women. According to Ellie Bosch it is just old wine in a new bottle (Bosch, 2002). It consists of a group of people of three to eight persons on the condition that each of them would be assuming responsibility for the development of all. Microfinance institution started in India in 1980s through Self Help Groups (SHGs) model. It is the Grameen replication model of Bangladesh.

MICROFINANCE, SHGs AND WOMEN EMPOWERMENT IN ANDHRA PRADESH

There is nearly 3,00,000 SHGs working all over India. The Ministry of Rural Development has special components for women in its programmes. Funds are earmarked as "Women's component" to ensure flow of adequate resources for the same. Projects and Schemes such as Swarnajayanthi Grameen Swarozgar Yojana (SGSY), Indira Awas Yojana, National Social Assistance Programme (NSAP), Restructured Rural Sanitation Programme, Accelerated Rural Water Supply Programme (ARWSP) the erstwhile Integrated Rural Development Programme (IRDP), the erstwhile Development of Women and Children in Rural Areas (DWCRA) and the Jowahar Rozgar Yojana (JRY).

The most successful region for microfinance is the southern part of India; Andhra Pradesh has become the example for the other states in this case. In Andhra Pradesh, various methods and schemes introduced for the women empowerment through self help groups. There are about 4.65 lakhs women SHGs in Andhra Pradesh covering nearly 61.70 lakhs poor women. Andhra Pradesh alone has about half of SHGs organized in the country. Various case studies show that there is a positive correlation between credit availability and women's empowerment. In Andhra Pradesh, all the villages in the state have at least one SHG and 75 per cent of the villages have 15-20 groups in each and each group consists of 15-20 members depend upon the group and area/ mandal.

Micro-Credit to SHGs

Micro-credit summit conducted in 1997 in Washington resolved to reach 100 million poor women by 2005 all over the world. In Andhra Pradesh alone, 61.70 lakh women were covered under micro-credit with a saving of a rupee per day and the financial institutions extending loans up to 4 times to the amount of group savings. Banks extending loans to SHGs and the recovery of loans is more than 95 per cent.

Economic empowerment of SHGs and impact of SHG movement

60 per cent of the women take up economic activities related to agriculture and allied activities. Land lease for growing agricultural crop is a common practice. Vegetable and flower cultivation food crops and pulses, oil-seed cultivation are taken up on leased lands. Similarly rearing of calves, ram lamb, chicks, piggery and duckery, dairy value addition to milk and milk products are preferred by women agricultural labourers. Illiterate and unskilled women engage in small

business activities. More than 15 per cent of the SHG members are artisans and engaged in making handloom products and handicrafts. In promoting economic opportunities to SHG members, Government has tie up with some private agencies, dealers for the sale of products manufactured by companies like Unilever Limited, TVS, TTK-Prestige, Colgate-Palmolive, Philips etc. Companies in return train SHGs in finance management, enterprise development, packaging, branding and pricing of products. This partnership is a win-win model. In Andhra Pradesh, SHGs are encouraged to get computers and software for accessing information and developing their business. Their products are photographed, scanned and displayed on websites. There are put on the portals of e-commerce companies. Handicrafts, herbal medicines and cosmetics, hand woven and embroidered curtains, toys, paintings etc., are thus finding national and international markets. This would not have been possible without internet access and computer knowledge. The members are enabled to take a mobile telephone and use it not only for the sales but as a public telephone.

EMPOWERMENT PROGRAMMES

Indira Kranthi Patham

The empowerment programmes are running in the name of Indira Kranthi Patham in A.P. An attempt has been made in analyzing how best the women benefited in microfinance with a study with reference to Chittoor district, Rayalaseema region of Andhra Pradesh.

Microfinance through Pavala Vaddi scheme

Microfinance through Pavala Vaddi scheme to SHGs in Andhra Pradesh, the Government of Andhra Pradesh has introduced Interest subsidy scheme w.e.f. July 1st, 2004. The objectives of the programme are:

1. Help reduce the financial burden on Self-Help Groups

2. Encourage groups to repay bank loans promptly
3. Help Bankers to achieve 100 per cent recovery under SHG-Bank Linkage Programme

Salient features of the scheme

1. All groups that have availed loans from banks under SHG-Bank Linkage Programme after 1st July 2004 are eligible for interest subsidy.
2. The groups should repay the loans as per the schedule negotiated with the banks.
3. In case any group is in default of interest/principal for more than three months, it becomes ineligible under the scheme.
4. Government has decided to bear the interest burden of groups over and above 3 per cent per annum charged by the bank.
5. Groups will have to regularly repay loan installments and interest to the bank.
6. Groups will not be required to obtain and submit any applications or certificates.
7. Government will make arrangements to remit the subsidy amount directly in the savings bank account of all eligible groups.

Need of the scheme

1. Self-Help movement of women with thrift as entry point has grown as a mass movement in Andhra Pradesh. There are about 6.99 lakh women Self-Help Groups covering nearly 89 lakh rural poor women in AP. The government adopted micro-credit as a tool to attain the economic empowerment of women and facilitated SHG bank linkage programme in a big way since 1998-99 onwards in the State. The SHG women have taken up various income generating activities by availing themselves of the facility under

the SHG-Bank Linkage programme and created a path for their economic empowerment. The Nationalized Banks, Regional Rural Banks and Co-operative Banks are coming forward to issue loan to Self-Help Groups.

2. The Banks are giving loans under SHG-Bank Linkage programme with different rates of interest ranging from 8 per cent to 12 per cent. The groups are facing difficulty in paying such rates of interest.
3. To reduce the financial burden of the Self Help Groups, the Government of Andhra Pradesh introduced the "Pavala Vaddi" scheme (Interest Subsidy) during the year 2004-05 with an objective to provide interest subsidy on the loans taken by Self-Help Groups under this scheme.

Process

1. The DRDA will obtain the details of SHG repayment for the purpose of interest subsidy twice a year through the Mandal Samakhyas.
2. DRDA will calculate the Pavala Vaddi to be given to each SHG basing on the bank statement. The DRDA will give the Pavala Vaddi Cheques to the Mandal Samakhya along with the statement of particulars accruing to each SHG.
3. The Mandal Samakhya in turn will distribute the cheques to the SHGs through the Village Organizations in the presence of non-officials.

In Chittoor district of Andhra Pradesh Pavala Vaddi Scheme succeeded in attaining the economic empowerment of women and facilitated SHG-Bank Linkage programme. Table 7.1 shows the microfinance–bank linkage pertaining to Chittoor district of Andhra Pradesh for the last five years.

Table 7.1: Microfinance SHG–bank linkage

Year	No. of SHGs	Amount (in crores)
2008-09	8273	129.63
2007-08	18269	250.69
2006-07	20198	196.04
2005-06	17296	119.34
2004-05	15676	72.53

In respect of Pavala Vaddi scheme as a part of Indira Kranthi Patham introduced in Chittoor district yields better results for the women empowerment. Pavala Vaddi loans and average sanctions per group in Chittoor district is tabulated in table 7.2.

Table 7.2: Particulars of Pavala Vaddi

Year	No. of SHGs	Pavala Vaddi loans	Average per group (in crores)
2008-09	8273	129.63	0.015
2007-08	18269	354.53	0.013
2006-07	20198	196.04	0.010
2005-06	17296	119.34	0.007
2004-05	15676	72.53	0.005

Table 7.3: Pavala Vaddi (interest subsidy)

Year	No. of groups	Pavala Vaddi amount released (in lakhs)	No. of SHG members
2008-09	3610	5.76	—
2007-08	27520	866.23	357760
2006-07	24999	418.27	287847
2005-06	10587	108.69	102542

Source: Notes for World Bank Mission, Oct-2008 IKP, DRDA, Chittoor

The subsidy amount released for groups of Chittor district shows how best the plan was introduced and implemented in Chittor district, A.P. The details are enumerated in table 7.3.

Total microfinance inclusion in Chitttor district for the financial years 2007-08 and 2008-09 is tabulated in table 7.4:

Table 7.4: Total financial inclusions

Year	No. of SHGs	Amount (in crores)
2008-09	881	29.43
2007-08	2084	72.41

Other schemes under Indira Kranthi Patham – Implementation in Chittoor district and its prospects.

Social Risk Management

Jana Sri Beema Yojana and other Group Insurance 2006-07

Under Social Risk Management Pilot initiatives, the Jana Sri Beema Yojana and Other Group Insurance schemes have been taken up in Chittoor district. The schemes were launched in May 2006 and commenced from 01/05/2006 with 1,26,150 members were enrolled, premium amount collected Rs. 63,07,500. 620 claims settled so far for an amount of Rs. 193.27 lakhs. Sanctioned scholarship for 16,509 pupils for an amount of Rs. 148.58 lakhs.

Jana Sri Beema Yojana and OGI 2007-08

- 3,36,163 SHG member have been enrolled in 65 mandals of the district with a premium amount of Rs. 165 each for a period of one year.
- So far 1843 death claims are received and being processed. 1771 death claims have been settled with an amount of Rs. 482.86 lakhs.
- 47,000 members claimed scholarships for the children studying IX class to senior inter and ITI for an amount of Rs. 405.00 lakhs from LIC of India.

Table 7.5: Coverage details

Event	Head of the family	SHG women
Natural death	Rs. 30,000	Rs. 10,000
Accidental death	Rs. 75,000	Rs. 20,000
Partial disability	Rs. 37,500	—
Permanent disability	Rs. 75,000	—

Aam Aadmi Beema Yojana

The scheme Aam Aadmi Beema Yojana (AABY) has been taken up in Chittoor district which was launched on 30th March 2008. In Chittoor district 1,74,957 members were enrolled and service charge collected 17,49,570 (Premium Rs. 200 paid by Central Govt and State Government (Rs. 100 + Rs. 100)

Table 7.6

Year	No. of enrolments	Total premium paid (service charge)	No. of claims settled	Amount (Rs. in lakhs)
2008-09	1,74,957	17,49,570	223	55.75

Cattle improvement through microfinance

- Chittoor distinct is famous for cow population from age-old days. The rural poor are having at least one cow in their backyard. This is the main economic activity taken up by rural women for their economic upliftment. They overcome their economic losses due to scanter rainfall and less yielding of agricultural crops. To strengthen the rural economic structure and to provide good rates to their milk and avoiding middlemen in the milk transactions the DPMU, Chittoor has established Bulk Milk Cooling Centers with Community involvement at all levels from milk procurement, processing to selling to big dairies.

- In Gangavaram and V. Kota the milk storage units have initiated and lot of improvement noticed in the lives of SHGs involved in it. Payment done to the milk producers till December 2008 is Rs. 61.70 crores.

Marketing initiatives in Chittoor district

To eliminate the unfair trade practices by local traders to enhance the bargaining power of the producers to ensure empowerment of women by collective marketing the initiatives are taken up in the district. The main object of marketing initiatives is to improve and diversify the sources of livelihoods and quality of life of the poor by increasing their incomes and providing wage days during lean days. In Chittoor district, Collective Procurement and Marketing of Non-Timber Forest Produce (NTFP) has yielded better results for needy ones.

Marketing strategy and approach

- The capacity of the community in managing the procurement center are developed by imparting training in two phases to VO/Ms procurement committee members, marketing CRPs, marketing assistants.
- As part of capacity building 175 village botanists, 45 marketing CRPs (mandals), 13 state marketing CRPs and marketing committee members are trained in collective procurement and marketing aspects.
- Trainings provided to NTFP collectors on sustainable collection to safeguard endangered spices.
- The three critical components required for collective procurement and marketing, i.e., infrastructure, working capital, training and capacity building are provided by supporting and strengthening the VOs and MS with working capital and CIF to purchase movable infrastructure like weighing scale, moisture meter, tarpaulin, sieving screen etc.

- Training is conducted on the process involved in procurement, storage disposal and importance of book-keeping, quality parameters, grading value addition, market fluctuations etc.
- The VOs have obtained fertilizer license and B class membership in Markfed.

Physical productive infrastructure

Weighing scales, moisture meters, tarpaulins, paddy cleaners, sieves are supplies to the Village Organizations (VO) for quality procurement. 16 godowns constructed in the district. Total Rs. 5.00 lakhs spent on physical infrastructure.

Progress made

Collected commodities like Decalips, Plumbago, Gachakayalu, Beeswax, Honey, Pongamia, Soapnuts, Hemidiscus, N.M Bark, Neem Seed, Neem Fruit, Cleaning Nuts, Nux Vomica, Gumbooruga, Gum Poliki Holestemma Adakodian, Emblica Officianalis, Celasia Reticulata Tinosora Cordifolia Euphorbia Anti Quorum Nalleru Gymnima Adathoda Vasica etc., are sold in the product demanding markets, for the

Table 7.7 NTFP Procurement Quantity and Value

Year	Qty procured in quintals	Value in lakhs	No. of Tribals benefited
2008	2850	25	4500
2007-08	6130	65	4500
2006-07	6440	72	4800
2005-06	7500	80	5500
2004-05	8742	93	5300
2003-04	7894	65	5200

No. of persons benefited with neem / pongamia—19500.
Total turnover from 2004-2008—Rs. 450 lakhs.
Total gross profit enjoyed VOs and MS around Rs. 50.00 lakhs.
Total tribals benefited—4500.

herbal and other medicinal products are usually sold at Chintamani of Karnataka State which is a boundary to Chittoor district.

Table 7.7 shows NTFP procurement quantity and value: Total Mandals 45 involved and Total No. of VOs involved are 175.

Apart from the above, there are other schemes such as land development, health and nutrition, employment generation, non-pesticide management, higher education, institutional building, village nirmita kendra which are implementing the scheems in Chittoor district with attractive results.

Fruits of microfinance and women empowerment through various schemes

Some success stories of women in SHGs of Chittoor district

In the struggle to achieve parity in life along with their menfolk, these women are gung-ho about their future. A case study of an individual in SHG from Chittoor (Rural) Mandal of A.P, reveals that after spending much of her time in hand-to-mouth existence and without two square meals per day, the story of R Ammulu (33) of Doddipalle village in Chittoor rural mandal comes across as an eye-opener. According to her, the entire family was dependent on the daily labour of Rs. 60 earned by her husband Rajender, who died of liver infection. But she didn't lose hope. After joining Vigna Vinayaka SHG (name given voluntarily by the SHG), she started earning Rs. 200 per day through her flour mill and by stitching clothes by having a microfinance by the government schemes. Moreover, at the same time, she didn't lose hope of the education of her children. Her daughter Sukanya and son Prasanth are studying in seventh and third classes respectively in a local school.

Another case of S Rama Devi, a poor illiterate of Etavakili village opined that though she did not enter a school, she ensured her two kids go to the government school, she herself involved and became a member of SHG and benefited from Indira Podupu Sangham, got a loan of Rs. 10,000 and purchased a cow a few years ago. She used to sell milk to private milk farms at Rs. 6 a litre. But with the advent of Bulk Milk Chillings Units (BMCUs), she now sells milk at Rs. 11-12, she says with pride. Stressing that the SHG concept has spelt wonders in their lives, Sridevi of Gurakambattu village claimed that the total finance inclusion plan has changed her life forever after her sangham received a loan of Rs. 4.7 lakh through Pavala Vaddi scheme. B V Ratna of Punganur in Chittoor district says microfinance and NREGA schemes have also helped them break new grounds and empowered them financially. Saying that the SHGs have given them a new lease of life, Shakaramma of Durga Velugu SHG in Kurabalakota and Anjalamma from Gauri SHG of Varadayapalem of Chittoor district, A.P. expressed that the women dairy farmers' efforts have paid dividends in Chittoor with the district topping the charts in BMCUs in the entire country. "The women are reaping huge profits now. There is no looking back now," she says. Shakaramma is a sprightly woman all of 56 years old.

Problems encountered and shortcomings noticed

1. *Burden of meeting*: Time consuming meetings, in particular in programmes based on group lending, and time consuming income generating activities without reduction of traditional responsibilities increase women's work and time burden.
2. Involvement of more than one family member in a single group gives lot of pressure on the family for repayment of installment, interest etc. which may ultimately lead to default of the SHG.
3. *New Pressures*: By using social capital, in-group lending/group collateral programmes, additional stresses and pressures are introduced, which might increase vulnerability and reflect disempowerment.

4. Credit policies that can gradually ruin their business (many customers cannot pay cash; on the other hand, suppliers are very harsh towards women).
5. *Reinforcement of traditional gender roles: lack of economic empowerment*: Microfinance assists women to perform traditional roles better and women thus remain trapped in low productivity sectors, not moving from the group of survival enterprises to micro-enterprises. There is evidence of men withdrawing their contributions to certain types of household expenditures.

Findings from the study

- 98 per cent of SHG members make savings regularly as the norms prescribed by the groups.
- All the groups meet at least once in a month to discuss various issues related to their day to day life, which helps and encourages sociological activities.
- 100 per cent children of SHG members are able to access immunization services against the diseases.
- Under Deepam scheme, promoted by Govt of A.P., 30 per cent of the members have access to safe cooking fuels (LPG), wherein gas connection will be given free of cost and the cylinder cost has to be borne by the member.
- 98 per cent of eligible members adopt small family norms.
- 80 per cent of the total SHGs have accessed financial assistance from banks and repayment is 98 per cent.
- Members are engaged in 450 varieties of income generating activities.
- Additional family incomes to members range from 1500-3000 per annum depending on the income generating activities.
- Increase in self-confidence and self-esteem.

- Increase in awareness levels about the society and community.
- Voluntary participation in community activities—laying roads, planting trees, conserving environment, construction of water harvesting structures, donations to the victims of natural calamities helping to reduce crime against girls and women. Campaign against eradication of social evils like dowry, child marriages, untouchability, AIDS, rescue and rehabilitations of orphaned children counseling SHG members learning from the past experiences are walking through the present are marching ahead for a bright future.

Conclusion and suggestions

Empowerment of women and the inculcation of financial training and discipline amongst the poor will undoubtedly have long-term socio-economic benefits. The principles of self-help and micro-credit thus hold the key to economic and socio-cultural freedom for India's millions of poor, opening the gates of a hitherto untapped reservoir of human enterprise.

- Marketing facilities for the sale of products of SHG may be introduced.
- Periodical exhibitions at block-level may be organised where the products of SHG can be displayed.
- Interactions among the groups to be encouraged by conducting meetings and seminars, where the members will get a chance to exchange their views and can strengthen their groups.
- Active intervention by district administration, professional bodies and voluntary organisations is precondition for the successful conception of micro-enterprises in terms of skill training, designing products, providing new technology and access to market.

- Members should be aware of legal literacy, rights and gender awareness. Trainings should be conducted in this regard by the mandal officers. The members should be given necessary training and guidance for the successful operation of the group.
- Members of the SHG should be more active, enthusiastic and dynamic to mobilise their savings by group actions. In this process NGOs should act as a facilitator and motivator.
- The office bearers managing the group should be given nominal financial benefits, which will enable them to be more involved in the activities of the Group and special incentives and perks also to be extended for them as a motivational tool and make them feel responsible and ambitious.
- The bank should extend adequate credit to the SHGs according to their needs. Cumbersome formalities should be made flexible and easy for the SHGs to operate the financial transactions.
- Uniformity should be maintained in formation and extension of financial assistance to them by banks in all blocks.

Government of Andhra Pradesh has rightly realized that the involvement of the rural poor women in development will spread up attainment of Swarna Andhra Pradesh and realizing the vision in deed.

REFERENCES

1. Kabeer, N. (2001), "Resources Agency Achievements: Reflections on the Measurement of Women's Empowerment–Theory and Practice", SIDA Studies, No. 3.
2. Kapoor, Pramilla (2001), *Empowering the Indian Women*, Publications Division, Ministry of Information and Broadcasting, Government of India.

3. Malhotra, Meenakshi (2004), *Empowerment of Women*, Isha Books, Delhi.

4. Ananta Basudev Sahu and Sandhya Rani Das – Research article on "Women Empowerment Through Self Help Groups—A Case Study."

5. Tiyas Biswas, "Women Empowerment Through Microfinance: A Boon for Development" – a research article

6. Harper, Malcolm, 2002, "Promotion of Self Help Groups under the SHG Bank Linkage Program in India", Paper presented at the Seminar on SHG-Bank Linkage Programme at New Delhi, November 25-26, 2002.

7. Bansal, Hema, 2003, "SHG-Bank Linkage Program in India: An Overview", *Journal of Microfinance*, Vol. 5, Number 1.

8. Rajesh Chakrabarti, "The Indian Microfinance Experience – Accomplishments and Challenges"–an article.

8

Microfinance in the Republic of Rwanda

Opportunities and Challenges

*Dr. V. Sundar
**Mbera R. Zenon

ABSTRACT

This article on "Microfinance in the Republic of Rwanda, Opportunities and Challenges" is based on the microfinance system in Rwanda. This paper tried to attempt to depict the opportunities and challenges in the country. One of the authors of the paper is a Rwandan citizen, hence this topic has been chosen for presentation in the Seminar. Rwanda is a small and landlocked country, located in the Eastern Africa. The country has 26,338 sq. km. of total area, of which 24,950 sq. km. or 94.7 per cent is made-up of land and 1,388 sq. km. or 5.3 per cent of water. However 32.7 per cent are suitable for cultivation.

In 2007, Rwandan population amounts to 9.9 million inhabitants, 60 per cent living below poverty line, and has a density of 311 inhabitants per sq. km. Ninety per cent of the population lives on agriculture-based activities. Before 1994, in Rwanda, apart from Popular Banks of Rwanda and some NGOs that offered

* M.Com., M.Phil., Ph.D., Reader in Commerce, Annamalai University, Annamalai Nagar-608 002.

** Ph.D., Research Scholar, Department of Commerce, Annamalai University.

financial services to the population, the microfinance did not experience a significant establishment. The microfinance sector had an increase of MFIs with a fabulous boom for the period between 2003 and 2005 characterized by the establishment of more than 80 institutions that joined Popular Banks of Rwanda network channeling deposits reaching about 30 billion Rwandan francs. Up to December 31st, 2007 licensed MFIs were 85. The government of Rwanda is aware that poverty reduction could not be achieved without access to financial services by the poor. As a result, microfinance is considered a powerful tool. A number of initiatives to boost the microfinance sector in Rwanda have been put in place so far, including the development of a legal and regulatory framework.

Following are the challenges: *Bad credit culture, weak MFI institutional capacity, skill level, ineffective MFI practitioner association, enabling and proper legal and regulatory environment, lack of donor coordination, No shared vision, undeveloped sector infrastructure, limited outreach in rural areas.*

Major opportunities are as follow: *High population density, important untapped market demand, potential to reach sustainability, Banking sector downscaling interest, manageable task.*

Introduction

This article on "Microfinance in the Republic of Rwanda: Opportunities and Challenges" is based on the microfinance system in Rwanda. This article tried to attempt to depict the opportunities and challenges in the country. One of the authors of the paper is a Rwandan citizen, hence this topic has been chosen for presentation in the Seminar.

Rwanda is a small and landlocked country, located in the Eastern Africa. The country has 26,338 sq. km. of total area, of which 24,950 sq. km. or 94.7 per cent is made-up of land and 1,388 sq. km. or 5.3 per cent of water. However 32.7 per cent are suitable for cultivation.

In 2007, Rwandan population amounts to 9.9 million inhabitants, 60 per cent living below poverty line, and has a density of 311 inhabitants per square kilometer. Ninety per cent (90%) of the population lives on agriculture based activities.

Definition and meaning in the context of Rwanda

Microfinance is often defined as financial services for poor and low-income group of people. In practice, the term is often used more narrowly to refer to loans and other services from providers that identify themselves as "Microfinance Institutions" (MFIs). These institutions commonly tend to use new methods developed over the last 30 years to deliver very small loans to unsalaried class of borrowers. These methods include group lending and liability, pre-loan savings requirements, and an implicit guarantee of ready access to future loans if present loans are repaid fully and promptly by the borrowers.

More broadly, microfinance refers to a movement that envisions a world in which low-income households have permanent access to a range of high quality financial services to finance their income-producing activities, build assets, stabilize consumption, and protect against risks. These services are not limited to credit, but include savings, Insurance, and money transfers. The Rwandan Microfinance sector consider loan less than 500,000 Rwf (38,000 INR), but more than 50,000 Rwf (3,800 INR) at 2 per cent interest monthly to unsalaried borrowers with monthly income less than 20,000 Rwf (1,600 INR) as microloan. Microfinance clients are poor and low-income people that do not have access to other formal financial institutions. Microfinance clients are usually self-employed, household-based entrepreneurs. Their diverse "micro-enterprises" include small retail shops, street vendors, rural artisans, and service providers. In rural areas, micro-entrepreneurs often have small income-generating activities such as food processing and trade.

However most of microfinance clients fall below the poverty line. The repayment period is up to 18 months.

The National household survey 2001, consider a man or a woman to be poor if their household has a total level of expenditure less than 64,000 Rwf (INR 5,000), or if their food expenditures fall below 45,000 Rwf (INR 3,500) per equivalent adult per annum, or if the household does not satisfy the basic needs (food, clothing, medical costs, children schooling etc.…)

Background of Rwandan microfinance

Before 1994, in Rwanda, apart from Popular Banks of Rwanda and some NGOs that offered financial services to the population, the microfinance did not experience a significant establishment. The microfinance sector had an increase of MFIs with a fabulous boom for the period between 2003 and 2005, characterized by the establishment of more than 80 institutions that joined Popular Banks of Rwanda network channeling deposits reaching about 30 billion Rwf. Up to December 31st, 2007 licensed MFIs were 85.

Improved financial services provide the poor an opportunity to improve their livelihood and, alongside with social services, can contribute to poverty reduction. The financial services needed do not cover micro-credit alone, but also other services are in demand. These include above all savings, but also money transfer services, micro-insurance and micro-leasing, all of which can play an important role in the economic empowerment of the poor.

The government of Rwanda is aware that poverty reduction could not be achieved without access to financial services by the poor. As a result, microfinance is considered as powerful tool. A number of initiatives to boost the microfinance sector in Rwanda have been put in place so far, including the development of a legal and regulatory framework.

Demand of microfinance

Before the 1994 war, Rwanda had a thriving micro-manufacturing sector, arts and crafts, carpentry, tailoring, garment making, metal working, leather products, minerals and maintenance work. The Ministry of Industry and Tourism undertook a survey in 2000 to determine the constraints of Small and Medium size Enterprises (SMEs). Entrepreneurs cited lack of finance (33%), followed by lack of qualified human resources (21%) as main business constraints.

The poor, in particular, have had very limited contact with financial institutions and are not used to accessing formal financial products. They are unaware of the range of the different financial products available. A survey conducted by the World Council of Credit Unions (WOCCU) with four credit unions in Rwanda revealed that approximately 50 per cent of clients and non-clients were not aware of the financial services provided by cooperatives. The Ministry of Finance (Minecofin) conducted a poverty assessment survey across the country that revealed that 77 per cent of potential microfinance clients have never resorted to any formal or informal financial services provider while 23 per cent had.

Table 8.1: Estimate of the low income active population without access to financial services

	Statistics	Calculation
Population size	8.8 million	
Active population	53%	4.6 million
Active population with access to financial services	21%	966,000
Active population without access to financial services	79%	3.6 million
In terms of population below poverty line	60%	2.1 million
In terms of households below poverty line	Average household size = 5.3	400,000 households

Source: Compiled from PRSP, Minecofin Census 2002, www.popcouncil.org/pdfs/wp/144.pdf

A recent financial sector assessment estimated that 15 per cent of the economically active population has a savings account in formal financial institutions. Though the percentage of the active population with access to finance is 21 per cent, hence a bit higher than the access to formal accounts, it still demonstrates that the majority of the Rwandese has to live without this basic service. Table 8.1 demonstrates that the number of households in need of microfinance and currently not serviced is 2.1 million people or about 400,000 households.

Uses of microfinance

The following are the most popular uses of microfinance services:

- Livestock (animal husbandry) and organic fertilizers.
- To take advantage of business opportunities.
- Agriculture or purchasing a piece of land.
- Construction and housing.
- Purchase raw materials.
- Business improvements or diversification.
- Purchase equipment.

The primary reasons for the use of microfinance services were reported to be: safety, easy access, interesting terms and conditions, proximity, speed, credit and affordable collateral requirements.

Despite their need for financial services, potential clients consider that the following factors hamper their capacity to use financial services: nepotism, risk aversion, lack of collateral, unfriendly terms and conditions, lack of trust in MFIs, bureaucracy and paperwork.

Interestingly, a detailed analysis of a sample of 350 credit union non-members in the cities of Gisenyi, Ruhengeri, Kigali, Gitarama and Butare revealed that monthly household expenses per capita equalled 15,878 Rwf (1,300 INR), while their household business income per capita was over 60,000 Rwf (4,700 INR). This suggests a significant positive liquidity capacity in the low income no served population. An increase in access of the poor clientele to reliable financial institutions and appropriate savings facilities could increase savings mobilization and help microfinance institutions better manage their liquidity stress.

Microfinance service providers

There has been an impressive growth of MFIs over the last three years. The Central Bank has a list of 107 MFIs and donor programs. There are over 600,000 clients served by MFIs, some estimates are as high as one million. However, these include agriculture input financing and various types of donor projects possibly including in-kind credit, which is normally not categorized as microfinance. Also included in the high figure are all estimated members of all saving and credit cooperative networks, of which usually only a portion of members are active savers or borrowers. Nevertheless, it is clear that the market penetration is higher in some other countries. In terms of volume, close to US $100 million is mobilized in the sector and $85 million was extended to MFI clients as credit. In comparison, the banking sector has approximately $400 million in deposits and slightly over $300 million in loans. These volumes speak for themselves, demonstrating the significance sector in the financial sector.

Table 8.2: Market penetration of MFIs in selected districts

Province	District	Population	MFI potential clients	Actual clients	Penetration
Kibuye	Budaha	46,674	38,287	00	00
Kibuye	Rusenyi	107,761	78,343	839	1%
Kibuye	Kibuye Town	44,363	21,399	6,051	28%
Butare	Maraba	66,983	35,500	2,893	8%
Butare	Save	66,393	39,097	2,130	5%
Butare	Kiruhura	68,007	38,528	00	00

Source: SNV Rwanda country position paper, 2005.

Table 8.2 shows for two provinces the variations in penetration per district. The variation can be explained as follows. Leading institutions are focused on increasing their market share and outreach by expanding geographically to cash crops zones and relatively developed regions. This is understandable, as MFIs are on the path towards sustainability, and need to become profitable to ensure their continued financial health and success. A few smaller sized institutions are considering a growth strategy geared towards underserved and remote areas where they could use a quasi-monopolistic position to increase their market share.

CHALLENGES AND OPPORTUNITIES

The following are the challenges the microfinance sector is facing in Rwanda.

Challenges

Bad credit culture

This bad credit repayment history stems from the international aid and donations influx after the 1994 war and mixing of loans and grants, which distorted the market. MFIs are still struggling to inculcate a repayment culture with their clients. This and limited employment of industry's best practices, contribute to the relative low portfolio quality encountered in Rwanda.

Weak MFI institutional capacity

Institutional capacity is weak in credit management, MIS and internal controls, business planning and market research and product development.

Skill level

MFIs find it challenging to recruit capable staff due to a low general skill level, which is not uncommon for post-conflict environments.

Ineffective MFI practitioner association

Microfinance network associations can potentially serve as a platform to bring together the different donor organizations, government ministries, supervisory authorities, MFIs and clients to share ideas and experiences, lessons learned, coordinate efforts and collaborations and serve as a self-regulatory entity. However, in Rwanda it is not spearheading the sector's development and formalization.

Enabling and proper legal and regulatory environment

The legal and regulatory framework's development has been work in progress since 2002 and remains a challenge to overcome. It is felt that there is a lack of categorization depending on the different types of existing MFIs and the types of services offered, such as small grassroot NGO's and larger MFI's with savings mobilization capacities. Additionally, the Central Bank currently does not yet have the human resource capacity to license and effectively implement appropriate prudential regulation for deposit taking institutions.

Lack of donor coordination

Donors are not working in a coordinated manner resulting in the duplication of efforts in a number of domains. There is also a lack of industry learning from past ineffective programming (association support, bank linkages, etc). The wheel is reinvented a lot and projects are working in silos from each other and are not geared towards the building of an inclusive financial sector and measuring of progress to this end.

No shared vision

Despite the government's clear engagement in microfinance, they have not yet managed to organize a broad dialogue among all stakeholders to agree on key sector constraints, priorities and an agenda to support the sector's healthy expansion.

Underdeveloped sector infrastructure

Sector support mechanisms such as technical assistance providers, credit bureaus, audit firms, research institutions, rating agencies, and linkages with business development services (BDS) providers are either non-existents or in the development phase, which hinders the sectors advancement. In particular, the opinions to choose from as technical service provider in Rwanda are rather limited, international NGO's such as AQUADEV, CARE, CRS and Trocaire provide training to partner MFIs, but such training or technical assistance is limited to a few weeks per year.

Limited outreach in rural areas

The lack of basic infrastructure in rural and remote areas (electricity, roads, etc.) is an impediment to MFIs expansion in those zones. Notably, MFIs are not connected to any kind of payment system which limits their capacity to expand their outreach. While the closure of weak MFIs is a direct and positive effect of the new regulatory framework, it also reduced the outreach in remote rural areas.

Opportunities

The assessment also identified the following major opportunities for the microfinance sector in Rwanda.

Important untapped market demand

The majority of the active poor population does not have access to financial services. This implies there is a large expansion and profit building margin for key market players.

High population density

This also is an opportunity for MFIs to increase their outreach with relatively low transaction costs.

Potential to reach sustainability

In view of the limited- though increasing- competition in the microfinance sector, most MFIs could still build up a significant market share and reach sustainability relatively easily.

Banking sector downscaling interest

The total MFI portfolio is large compared to the formal banking sector's portfolio. As a result, banks are reviewing their loan products and have become interested in including MFIs as a lending client. This would mean more sustainable wholesale finance than guarantee facilities, government or donor projects.

Manageable task

Rwanda is a small country, and the building of an inclusive financial sector is rather manageable, and much easier than in vast countries like Nigeria, with more complex administrative structures and regulations.

Conclusion

In Rwanda, Microfinance is in juvenile stage. It has to grow more. The purpose of microfinance in Rwanda is to improve the socio-economic status of the people who are living under the poverty line. However, the Microfinance sector is facing many challenges. The only way of improving the microfinance sector in Rwanda is to face the challenges and make a financial service menu accessible by any bankable Rwandan. This needs a national level administration policy decisions. If this is done, this may help the rural poor to improve their standard of life and Microfinance sector in the country of Rwanda.

REFERENCES

1. African Development Bank, Rwanda, "Evaluation of the Banks Assistance to the social Sector," Sept 2002.
2. Word Bank, Rwanda (www.worldbank.org)
3. IMF, Rwanda Financial Sector Assessment, 2005.
4. Ministry of Finance Census 2002, Rwanda.
5. World Council of Credit Unions (WOCCU), 2002.
6. National Bank of Rwanda, Annual report on Bank supervision (1995- 2007)
7. www.bnr.rw.

9

Impact of Microfinance on Provision of Employment and Income Generation for Women Members of Self-Help Groups

A Study in Indukurpet Mandal, Nellore District, A.P.

*K. Pavani Reddy
**K. Vijayalakshmi

ABSTRACT

Women in India have been traditionally suppressed and particularly women belong to the economically and socially weaker sections of the society even more impressed. It was very needed to reduce poverty and empower women. Micro-credit is now seen as one of the very promising types of intervention to reduce poverty and empower women. The Self-Help-Groups have been addressing on specific problems by collective action.

Ours is a male-dominated society, where women are described as the 'second sex and the second creature' who live on surplus. Their very existence has been considered as parasite on the men who rule them. Female subordination has been an essential feature of human life in all contemporary societies, although

* MHRM Student, Y. V. University, Kadapa-516003
** MHRM Student, Y. V. University, Kadapa-516003

with a varying degree and expression of male dominance. All the provisions in the Constitution and the spate of legislations encased to empower women in the post-Independent India have not been adequate to set women free from their traditional bondages, liabilities and restrictions. Even today women's participations in the decision-making processes, especially in the rural areas has remained very marginal. The Noble Laureate, Professor Amartya Sen has rightly emphasized the need to view women as "potentially active agents of social change and to transcend the view of women as patient solicitors of social equity". Hence, there is a need to involve rural women in income-generating economic activities. Development of women has been considered a sine-qua-non *for national development and social welfare.*

Introduction

Ours is a male-dominated society, where women are described as the 'second sex and the second creature' who live on surplus. Their very existence has been considered as parasite on the men who rule them. Female subordination has been an essential feature of human life in all contemporary societies, although with a varying degree and expression of male dominance. Women in India have been traditionally suppressed and particularly women belong to the economically and socially weaker sections of the society have been even more impressed. All the provisions in the Constitution and the spate of legislations encased to empower women in the post-Independent India have not been adequate to set women free from their traditional bondages, liabilities and restrictions. Even today women's participations in the decision-making processes, especially in the rural areas has remained very marginal. The Noble Laureate, Professor Amartya Sen has rightly emphasized the need to view women as "potentially active agents of social change and to transcend the view of women as patient solicitors of social equity". Hence, there is a need to involve rural women in income-generating economic activities. Development of women has been considered a *sine-qua-non* for national development and social welfare. Government has launched several developmental programmes for women with a view to bringing them into the mainstream of the economy and the society by generating employment and income. With the exclusive objective, the government of India launched special poverty alleviation programme like 'Development for Women and Children in Rural Areas (DWCRA) for women in 1982-83, as a sub-component of 'Integrated Rural Development Progarmme' (IRDP).

MICROFINANCE

In India various Five-Year Plans gave special emphasis to the activities of employment and income for women with the ultimate objective of making women economically independent and self-reliant. In spite of efforts made by the government, women needs are more and more marginalized in their struggle for existence and excellence. The credit requirements of poor and women are not met by the formal banking. Women are driven to status of recipient, beneficiary and consumer, despite their ability as a giver, benefactor and producer. In these circumstances evolved the concept of micro-credit.

Micro-credit plays a crucial role in the poverty reduction strategies in many countries. Micro-credit, according to Weber, "differs significantly from other targeted poverty reduction strategies in that it is enable in a commercial framework" and reinforces norms regarding repayment in commercial transactions, contracts etc. Micro-credit is now seen as one of the very promising types of intervention to reduce poverty and empower women.

The self-help groups are formed for the development of poor rural women through the provision of micro-credit provided by the banking sector. The Reserve Bank of India has launched the programme of linking self-help groups with lending institutions like commercial banks, so that the requirements of self-help groups can be properly attempted by the banks. Along with the self-help groups non-governmental organizations also play a crucial role in obtaining the micro-credit by the rural poor.

A self-help group may be defined as a voluntary group village personal interaction and perceived as alterable, pressing and personal by most as its members. According to NABARD, "it is a homogeneous group of rural poor voluntary formed to save whatever amount they can conveniently save of their earnings and mutually agree to contribute to a common fund of the group to be lent to the members for meeting their productive and emergent credit needs." It may be defined commonly as 'a group of ten to twenty members, usually poor women who pool their savings into a fund from which they can borrow as and when necessary. These groups deposits their savings with a local bank. The government has recognized this SHGs strategy that will bring up poor rural women from below the poverty line by providing financial assistance through sparing and government agencies.

ORIGIN OF SHGs

The establishment of SHGs could be traced as existence of one or more common problem areas around which the consciousness of the rural poor was built and process of group formation initiated. Thus the group was usually responsive to perceived need. Such groups have been formed around specific production activities and often they have the promoted savings among their members and used the pooled resources to meet the emergent needs. Sometimes the internal savings generated were supplemented by the external resources loaned / donated by promoting the SHGs. Since the SHGs have been able to mobilize savings and also to recycle effectively the pooled resources amongst the members their activities have attracted attention as a supportive mechanism for meeting the credit needs of the poor. After formation of the SHGs, in order to strengthen the functioning of the SHGs at grassroot level the government encourages the formation of 'Sangamitra Groups' in every village. The same trend has been found in the case of 'Sangamitra Groups' also.

SELF-HELP MOVEMENT IN ANDHRA PRADESH

Since 1970, developing countries have been increasing focus on self-help groups through non-governmental organization to facilitate the access of poor women households to financial services like credit, savings and thrifts etc. Self-help groups as a sub-scheme of Integrated Rural Development Programme (IRDP) started in Andhra Pradesh in 1982-83 with UNICEF co-operation with the primary objective of focusing attention on women members of rural families below the poverty line with a view to generate self-employment on the sustained basis. The SHGs movement gathered momentum in 1993 in Andhra Pradesh. The women in Nellore district had been organized in to 'Mahila Mandals' (women associations) during total literacy campaign (TLC) in 1992. Subsequently these groups spread as anti-arrack (abolish of country-made liquor) movement. The movement was successful and widespread to the neighbouring districts, eventually leading to imposition of prohibition in the state. Water movement converted into savings and credit groups known as 'Podupu Lakshmi' (saving money) by the NGOs and 'Mahila Mandals'. These Podupu Lakshmi groups were converted in to DWACRA self-help groups by the department of Child and Women Development of government of Andhra Pradesh. The government of Andhra Pradesh has reorganized self-help approach as an effective strategy to tackle socio-economic problem of poverty especially amongst women. The World Bank Micro-Credit Summit held in Washington in 2001-02 has agreed that women's self-help is one of the most important schemes to eliminate the socio-economic poverty.

Role of SHGs

The SHGs are playing a crucial role in social, economic and educational strategies in India especially in Andhra Pradesh. The SHGs have been addressing local specific social problems by collective action like shut down of belt shops (liquor shops), child marriages, trafficking of domestic women/girls and gambling, in eradicating dowry, on corruption in public officials and public distribution system. The SHGs are contributing also to education by conducting 'Mid-Day-Meals' programme. Besides their micro-credit activities with the support of micro-credit the members of SHGs have been involving collectively in number of economic activities which fetch them more remunerative returns.

Statement of the problem

Government of Andhra Pradesh has been encouraging the Self-Help Group movement as an instrument to create employment opportunities for rural women as a part of the programme. After implementation of the programme, there is a spectacular increase in the number of SHGs and their members in the state. The cumulative savings and loans outstandings have reached to Rs. 32 crores and Rs. 5610 crores respectively. The average loan amount per member is higher (Rs. 13510) in Andhra Pradesh as compared to rest of the states in India. Though there were several studies saying positive impact of micro-credit schemes on employment and income generation of the rural women in general, these fruits of micro-credits have not reached to the Scheduled Castes and Scheduled Tribes women members. So, the problem is whether the Bank-SCs/STs-SHGs linkage has properly done? Whether the weaker sections particularly SCs/STs SHGs get their due share in total corpus fund, loan amounts micro-credit under Bank-SHGs linkage programme? Are they really got out of the cruel clutches of rural moneylenders after availing micro-credit? Most of the studies both at micro- and macro-level did not touch upon these issues mostly relating to SCs/STs women SHGs. Even the NABARD's evaluation studies could not able to study the functioning of SCs/STs SHGs and their bank linkage programme and the impact of micro-credit on employment and income generation and asset creation of SCs/STs women beneficiaries of SHGs in sample districts of Andhra Pradesh where about 28 per cent of SHGs are concentrated and functioning at grassroot level.

Objectives

The main objective of the study is to study the impact of micro-credit on employment and income generation and asset creation of rural women members of SHGs.

Methodology

It was fulfill the above objective by using the paired t-test statistic.

There are some situations, which we have dependent samples. Two samples are said to be dependent when the elements in one sample are related to those in the other in any significant or some meaningful manner.

For example, advertisement effect on sales of a product before and after (or) efficiency of drugs before and after its use.

In analyzing the effects, we oftenly use paired t-test statistic. The test statistic is

$$|t| = \frac{\bar{d}}{S.D.\sqrt{n-1}} \sim\rightarrow t_{(n-k)}$$

where,

$\bar{d}$ = the mean of difference

d = the difference between paired samples

σ = the standard deviation of difference.

Limitations of the study

The study confines itself to study the impact of micro-credits on the sample women members of SHGs in the Indukurpet mandal in Nellore district in the year 2007-08. The data for the study has been collected through interview method. Since the most of beneficiaries do not maintain proper accounts and most of them are illiterates and they are possibilities of statistical and hence data collected would only be in approximation to actual facts.

ANALYSIS

Micro-credit means the extension of small loans to very poor people for self-employment projects that generate income, allowing them to care for themselves and their families. In most cases, micro-credit programmes offer a combination of services and resources to their clients in addition to credits for self-employment. These often include saving facilities, training, networking and peer support. Loans under micro-credit programme are very small, on an average less than $100 by world standards and in hundreds of rupees by Indian standards. Micro-credit targets the rural and urban households, with an emphasis on women borrowers, provisions of finance for creation of assets and their main tenancy and bringing in greater quality of services. The beneficiaries are identified by micro-credit providers themselves independently or through self-help groups. The SHGs mechanism has been widely accepted as an integral part of microfinance.

Village-wise institutional provision of micro-credit

In the study area of Indukurpet mandal, there were six sample villages taken i.e., Indukurpet, Komarika, Laburu, Mypadu, Nidimusali and Pallipadu. The Nidimusali village is mobilized about 30 per cent of total saving followed by Komarika (24%), Pallipadu (18%) and Mypadu (17%) respectively. The SHGs in Indukurpet and Laburu villages have mobilized very small amount of saving—6 per cent. The women members of SHGs in Nidimusali are comparatively richer with original sources of irrigation and involving small scale and cottage industry. The corpus fund is provided

Table 9.1: Village-wise Micro-Credit (in Rs.)

S. No.	Village	Total savings thefts	Corpus fund	Bank loan	Total micro-credit
1.	Indukurpet	2100 (6.3)	22000 (15.7)	45000 (13.2)	69100 (12.5)
2.	Komarika	8000 (24.1)	17000 (12.9)	80000 (23.4)	115000 (20.9)
3.	Laburu	1950 (5.9)	21000 (15.0)	44000 (12.9)	66950 (12.1)
4.	Mypadu	5500 (16.6)	25000 (17.9)	47000 (13.7)	113600 (20.6)
5.	Pallipadu	5800 (17.5)	22000 (15.8)	60000 (17.5)	87800 (15.9)
6.	Nidimusali	9800 (29.6)	23000 (16.4)	66000 (19.3)	98800 (17.9)
Total		**33150 (100)**	**140000 (100)**	**342000 (100)**	**603750 (100)**

Note: Figures in parentheses are percentages to total figure.

commonly to all members on equal basis. So, that the corpus fund varies from 13 to 18 per cent among all the villages. In the view of the bank loan among the all villages, the Komarika village received large amount of bank loan (23%) as followed by Nidimusali (19%), Pallipadu (17.5%), Mypadu (14%) and Indukurpet and Laburu villages have received 13 per cent of bank loan as micro-credit. The Komarika received the highest micro-credit (21%) followed by Mypadu (20%), and Nidimusali (18%) whereas the lowest micro-credit is available in Laburu (12%) followed by Indukurpet (13%) and Pallipadu (16%) in the study area. The above analysis expressed that the societies which are very prompt in the repayment of loans are obtaining repeated and higher amount of the SHGs bank linkage programme.

Village-wise employment generation of SHGs

The main strategy of the SHGs movement is to improve the access of poor women to employment, skill training, credits and other financial supportive services. Microfinance institutions which provide credits for the SHGs are important vehicles for credits delivery, especially to self-employed persons, because of low cost of operation, high and assured returns. The impact of micro-credit on employment generation of poor women is very high in rural areas. The regional variation in terms of employment generation is prevalent in the study area. Some villages like, Nidimusali and Pallipadu are endowed with fertile and irrigation facilities. Laburu village is comparatively a backward village. The average employment generation of SHGs in the study area is shown in the below table 9.2.

Table 9.2: Village-wise employment generation of SHGs (in Rs.)

S. No.	Village	Pre-SHGs	Post-SHGs	Employment Increment	t-test
1.	Indukurpet	362.5	237.8	124.7	18.79
2.	Komarika	315.3	192.6	122.7	32.19*
3.	Laburu	374.4	291.0	83.4	14.01
4.	Mypadu	330.5	209.0	121.5	53.0*
5.	Pallipadu	407.45	226.7	180.75	64.8*
6.	Nidimusali	402.2	227.0	175.2	72.7*

*Significant at 0.05 probability level.

The table 9.2 shows that the average employment generation in the post-SHGs period is higher in Pallipadu village followed by Nidimusali and Mypadu villages. There is a significant increase in the income of the study area. So, the above analysis shows that the impact of SHGs on employment generation is positive in the study area.

Village-wise income generation of SHGs

Indukurpet mandal is highly developed one in Nellore district. In fact, the women of SHGs in the study area have been involved in various economic activities. Hence, their average income levels varies from one village to another village in post-SHGs period as shown in table 9.3.

Table 9.3: Village-wise income generation of SHGs (in Rs.)

S. No.	Village	Pre-SHGs	Post-SHGs	Income increment	t-test
1.	Indukurpet	10432.3	22146.4	11714.1	19.28
2.	Komarika	8830.4	20685.6	11855.2	36.02*
3.	Laburu	11867.0	23759.8	11892.8	27.81
4.	Mypadu	12858.4	26283.6	13425.2	42.3*
5.	Pallipadu	9995.9	26757.9	16762.0	49.18*
6.	Nidimusali	14772.0	36680.9	21909.0	69.42*

*Significant at 0.05 probability level.

The values given in table 9.3, expresses that the highest increase in income is found in Nidimusali village followed by Pallipadu, Mypadu, Laburu, Komarika and Indukurpet villages respectively in the study area. However, the percentage change in average increase in income is very low in Laburu village when compared to rest of the villages in the study area. There is a significant increase in income in Nidimusali, Pallipadu, Mypadu and Komarika villages in Indukurpet mandal of Nellore district. So, the impact of SHGs on income generation is positive in the study area.

Impact of SHGs in Indukurpet Mandal

The SHGs are having been formed to uplift living conditions of rural women who are below the poverty line. There was a strong impact of SHGs on women in views not in economically but also in sociologically and educationally in the study area (Indukurpet Mandal). Due to SHGs the confidence, lifestyle and living standards of the women have improved, who have membership with self-help groups.

Findings and suggestions

In the view of employment generation of SHGs, the average employment generation in the post-SHGs period is higher in Pallipadu village followed by Nidimusali and Mypadu villages. There is a significant increase in the income of the study area. Though there was increase in employment generation of SHGs, in most of the villages in Indukurpet mandal there is no significant increase. So, it is suggested to improve income conditions for women by increasing micro-credit and providing credit without interest to the SHGs with the help of nationalized banks by improving bank-SHGs linkage.

In the view of income generation of SHGs, the highest income increase is found in Nidimusali village followed by Pallipadu, Mypadu, Laburu Komarika and Indukurpet villages respectively in the study area. There is a significant increase in income in Nidimusali, Pallipadu, Mypadu and Komarika villages in Indukurpet mandal of Nellore district. Though there was increase in income generation of SHGs members, in more of the villages in Indukurpet mandal there is no significant increase. So, it is suggested to improve the employment conditions to improve the income of women by increasing micro-credit to the SHGs with the help of nationalized banks by improving bank-SHGs linkage. To fulfill the above said suggestions, the state government of Andhra Pradesh and its local bodies should take more care to improve bank-SHGs linkage.

REFERENCES

1. Kalbagh, *Women and Development*, Discovery Publishing House, New Delhi, 1992.
2. K.G. Kamarkar, *Rural credit and Self-Help-Groups' Microfinance Needs and Concepts in India*, Sage Publications, New Delhi, 1999.

3. Francin R. Frankel, *India Political Economy 1947-2004*, Oxford University Press, Bombay, 1998.
4. Ashok Kumari, *Development of Women and Children in India*, Common wealth Publishers, New Delhi, 1990.
5. Thomas Fisher and M.S. Sriram, *Beyond micro-credit putting development back into microfinance*, Vistaar Publications, New Delhi, 2004.
6. Dr. R. Suneetha "Is DWACRA Programme Empowering the Rural Women?" *Kurukshetra*, Vol. 55.
7. Agnihotri, S.P., *National Employment Programmes in India*, Chough Allahabad, 1992.

10

Women Empowerment through SHGs

A Special Focus on Kadapa District

*Dr. D. Sudarsana Murthy
**Dr. P.V. Narasaiah

ABSTRACT

India is having more than 100 crores of population, women share equal in ratio having 496 million, that is 48 per cent to the total population. The economic status of the women is generally poor which is a matter of great concern. The rural women directly or indirectly put their entrepreneurial skill in all rural employed activities such as agriculture operations, poultry, sheep rearing, dairy, sale of agricultural produce etc. Though they put their heart and soul in rural employment activities, their economic status is not improved. Even though they have entrepreneurial skills, due to poor financial strength they need financial assistance. Hence, the need for designing exclusive self-employment and other developmental programmes for promotion of women entrepreneurship was greatly stressed. The government has been implementing various programmes to provide self-employment opportunities to unemployed

* Associate Professor of Management, Sri Venkateswara Institute of Science and Technology, Kadapa-516 003

** Associate Professor of Commerce, Sri Venkateswara University, Tirupati-517 502

including women. Among them Self-Help Groups (SHGs) playing a significant role. The SHG growth which has almost assumed the form of a movement represents a massive grassroots level mobilization of poor rural women to small informal associations capable of forging links with formal systems to help access financial and other services needed for their socio-economic advancement.

Keeping in view the significance of SHGs in augmenting the entrepreneurial skills among women, the present study has been undertaken to evaluate the implementation of SHGs scheme in Kadapa district, a drought prone and backward district in the state of Andhra Pradesh. The study is confined to the woman beneficiaries. Secondary data with regard to status in number of beneficiaries, social strata and bank linkage are collected from the authentic records of the DRDA, Kadapa. In addition field study has been conducted to collect primary data with regard to the problems of women beneficiaries collected through pre-tested schedules.

To conclude, the awareness in rural areas among women belong to weaker sections is still limited. In addition, a major area of difficulty for women entrepreneur is that of marketing. Hence, strategies should be formulated to inculcate marketing skills and to enable the women entrepreneurs to sell their products with ease. The government has to make efforts for providing marketing facilities by opening various marketing stalls and exhibitions etc. Another major problem on part of women entrepreneurs is restrictive loan policies of the banks. The banks took long time to clearly recognize and internalize the concept. Some of the banks in the district were forcing the beneficiaries to pledge properties as collateral securities.

Introduction

India is having more than 100 crores of population, women share equal in ratio having 496 million, that is 48 per cent to the total population. The economic status of the women is generally poor which is a matter of great concern. The rural women directly or indirectly put their entrepreneurial skill in all rural employed activities such as agriculture operations, poultry, sheep rearing, dairy, sale of agricultural produce etc. Though they put their heart and soul in rural employment activities, their economic status is not improved. Even though they have entrepreneurial skills, due to poor financial strength they need financial assistance. Hence, the need for designing exclusive self-employment and other developmental programmes for promotion of women entrepreneurship was greatly stressed.

The government has been implementing various programmes to provide self-employment opportunities to un-employed including women. Among them Self-Help Groups (SHGs) playing a significant role. The SHG growth, which has almost assumed the form of a movement, represents a massive grassroots level mobilization of poor rural women to small informal associations capable of forging links with formal systems to help access financial and other services needed for their socio-economic advancement. Basically, SHGs are being promoted as a part of the microfinance interventions aimed at helping the poor to obtain easily financial services like savings, credit and insurance.

Self-Help Groups (SHGs): An overview

The promotion of SHGs in India begun more formally in 1992 with the launch of the SHG-Bank Linkage Programme by National Bank for Agricultural and Rural Development (NABARD). The main aim of the programme is to improve rural poors' access to formal credit system in a cost-effective sustainable manner by making use of SHGs which cover all economically viable activities including agriculture and allied activities. The normal bank rate of interest shall be charged, it may be between 9 to 11 per cent. On 1st July 2004, 0.25 paise interest rate came into existence.

Rationale of the study

Keeping in view the significance of SHGs in augmenting the entrepreneurial skills among women, the present study has been undertaken to evaluate the implementation of SHGs scheme in Kadapa district, a drought prone and backward district in the state of Andhra Pradesh. The study is confined to the woman beneficiaries. Secondary data with regard to status in number of beneficiaries, social strata and bank linkage are collected from the authentic records of the DRDA, Kadapa. In addition field study has been conducted to collect primary data with regard to the problems of women beneficiaries collected through pre-tested schedules.

Status of SHGs

Table 10.1 discloses the details with regard to number of groups formed from 2004-05 to 2007-08.

Table 10.1: Year-wise status of SHGs formed in Kadapa district

Year	No. of groups cumulative since inception	New groups
2004-2005	18000	—
2005-2006	24600	6600
2006-2007	28455	3855
2007-2008*	32610	4155

*Upto 9th Sept. 2007

Source: Data compiled from the records of DRDA, Kadapa.

It is observed that the number of women beneficiaries under SHGs increased from 18000 in 2004-05 to 32610 during 2007-08, constituting more than 80 per cent growth rate. However, the year-wise growth rate is sluggish.

Social status

Table 10.2 reflects the caste-wise details of women SHGs.

It is evident from the table 10.2 that majority of the women beneficiaries belong to O.C. category followed by B.C. category. Minorities are very low because of existence of various social problems. The downtrodden and retarded sections like SC and ST are fewer in number. This may be due to un-favourble economic, political, social and administrative conditions.

Table 10.2: Caste-wise classification of women beneficiaries

Caste	2004-05	2005-06	2006-07	2007-08
O.C.	6254 (34.74)	8215 (33.39)	9870) (34.68	10960 (33.61)
B.C.	5925 (32.92)	7820 (31.79)	9012 (31.67)	10497 (32.19)
S.C.	3423 (19.02)	4975 (20.02)	6841 (24.04)	7396 (22.68)
S.T.	612 (3.4)	842 (3.42)	862 (3.29)	7396 (22.68)
Minorities	1786 (9.92)	2.798 (11.38)	1870 (6.32)	2854 (8.75)
Total	**18000 (100)**	**24600 (100)**	**28455 (100)**	**32610 (100)**

Source: Same as in Table 10.1.
Note: Figures in parentheses represent percentage to total.

Bank Linkage Programme

In this scheme loans are deployed to women beneficiaries by banks on the recommendation of DRDA authorities. Table 10.3 manifests the number of women SHGs and loans sanctioned to them from 2004-05 to 2007-08.

Table 10.3: Coverage of SHGs and the amount sanctioned by various banks in Kadapa district

Year	No. of SHGs	Amount sanctioned (Rs. in lakhs)
2004-05	5426	3142
2005-06	10600	7245
2006-07	12526	10274
2007-08*	5965	8094

*Upto 5th September 2008.
Source: Same as in table 10.1.

The number of SHGs under bank linkage programme increased from 5426 in 2004-05 to 12526 in 2006-07 and 5965 SHGs have been covered upto 5th September, 2008. It is expected that this number would go up by 13,000 by the end of December, 2008. The credit deployment by banks to SHGs has registered an increasing trend. During the year 2004-05, an amount of Rs. 3142 lakhs was sanctioned by various banks in the district, which substantially rose to Rs. 10,274 lakhs by the end of 2006-07. A considerable amount, i.e., Rs. 8,094 was sanctioned by the banks upto 5th September, 2008. It is expected that this amount would increase by Rs. 14,000 lakhs by the end of the year 2007-08.

Bank-wise break up

Table 10.4 depicts the bank-wise participation in financing SHGs in the district.

Table 10.4: Amount sanctioned by banks to SHGs

(Rs. in lakhs)

Sl. No.	Name of the Bank	2004-05	2005-06	2006-07	2007-08
1.	Andhra Bank	125.09	276.04	350.07	239.61
2.	Central Bank of India	50.00	0.40	85.00	—
3.	Canara Bank	0.70	0.14	0.90	—
4.	Corporation Bank	29.11	83.26	118.15	142.34
5.	Indian Bank	0.15	7.00	5.00	—
6.	Punjab National Bank	50.00	1.75	0.31	—
7.	Andhra Pragathi Grameena Bank	1839.13	4472.87	5821.09	4452.54
8.	State Bank of Hydrabad	2.76	3.17	4.96	6.02
9.	State Bank of India	677.41	1701.64	2660.80	2446.85
10.	Syndicate Bank	356.73	683.26	1187.17	723.48
11.	Union Bank of India	4.80	7.70	14.55	7.80
12.	The Ing Vysya Bank	6.75	8.20	23.25	78.11
	Total	**3142.63**	**7245.43**	**10274.06**	**8094.08**

It is evidenced from the table 10.4 that Andhra Pragathi Grameena Bank captured first place among all the banks in credit deployment to the SHGs and followed by State Bank of India and Syndicate Bank. As a rural bank, AGB has been instrumental for developing women entrepreneurs by providing adequate credit.

Impediments/Challenges of women entrepreneurs

In order to identify the major problems encountered by women entrepreneurs of SHGs, 75 women beneficiaries have been selected at random. The selection is based on the list of women beneficiaries supplied by DRDA, Kadapa. Table 10.5 focuses on the major problems encountered by the sample respondents. Almost all the respondents reported multiple problems.

Table 10.5: Problems reported by women SHGs

Sl.No.	Problems	No. of respondents	% to total*
1.	Personal problems	43	57
2.	Education problems	33	44
3.	Social problems	30	40
4.	Economic/Financial problems	50	67
5.	Technological problems	25	33
6.	Raw material problems	35	47
7.	Marketing problems	55	73
8.	Manpower support problems	30	40
9.	Competition from large firms	38	51
10.	Bureaucratic delay in getting payments from government departments	35	47

*Multiple Responses

Source: Field survey

It is apparent from the table 10.5 that large numbers of respondents (55) have reported marketing as a major problem. Next to marketing, financial problems have been reported by 50 respondents, constituting 67 per cent of the sample size. The rest of the respondents complained competition from personal, large firms, social disparities etc., as other major problems seriously affecting their units.

Concluding remarks

To conclude, the awareness in rural areas among women belong to weaker sections is still limited. In addition, a major area of difficulty for women entrepreneur is that of marketing. Hence, strategies should be formulated to inculcate marketing skills and to enable the women entrepreneurs to sell their products with ease. The government has to make efforts for providing marketing facilities by opening various marketing stalls and exhibitions etc. Another major problem on part of women entrepreneurs is restrictive loan policies of the banks. The banks took long time to clearly recognize and internalize the concept. Some of the banks in the district were forcing the beneficiaries to pledge properties as collateral securities.

Majority of the women beneficiaries are not completely aware of the procedure of SHG scheme. The DRDA and banks have to conduct awareness programmes to improve awareness among rural women. SHG members have often lacked business skills and administrative capacity due to the inadequate provision of education and training. It is, therefore, essential on part of the members. Hence, the government organs like DRDA and banks have to provide training facilities. In this regard, the non-government organizations and other associations should take initiative to make the women aware and motivate them towards self-employment. Further, women should be encouraged to start ventures confidently with enthusiasm by employing modern technology. They have to shift their line of activities on scientific and modern lines. The government should ensure a speedy change from traditional occupation to modern business enterprises in order to take the maximum benefit of new market conditions and technology. These measures, no doubt would certainly change traditional women and mould them as omnipotent.

REFERENCES

1. Gardon E., and K. Natarasan., *Entrepreneurship Development*, Himalaya Publishing House, 2003.
2. Goetz., Anne Marie., *Women Development Workers, implementing rural credit programmes in Bangladesh*, Sage Publications, New Delhi, 2001.
3. Satya Sundaram, I., *Rural Development*, Himalaya Publishing House, New Delhi, 2002.
4. Ajaha, R.K., "Self Help Groups and Rural Employment," *Yojana*, April, 2001.
5. Note on self-employment schemes in Kadapa District, DRDA, Kadapa.

11

Microfinance and Women Empowerment through Pavala Vaddi Strategy

*Dr. B. Amarnath
**Dr. S. Raghunatha Reddy
***Mr. Thulasi Krishna, K.

Introduction

The non-availability of credit and banking facilities to the poor and under-privileged segments of the society has always been a major concern in India. Accordingly, both, the Government and the Reserve Bank, have taken several initiatives, from time to time, such as nationalisation of banks, prescription of priority sector lending norms and concessional interest rate for the weaker sections. It was, however, realised that further direct efforts were required to address the credit needs of the poor. In response to this requirement, the concept of microfinance movement has evolved in India in early 1990s.

The term microfinance is of recent origin and is commonly used in addressing the issues related to poverty alleviation (make easy), financial support to micro-entrepreneurs,

---

* Associate Professor, Department of Management Studies, S.V. University, Tirupati.
** Associate Professor, Kandula School of Management, Kadapa.
*** Research Scholar, Department of Management Studies, S.V. University, Tirupati.

gender development etc. Microfinance is the provision of thrift, credit and other financial services and products of very small amounts to the poor to enable them to raise their income levels and improve their living standards. It has been recognised that microfinance helps the poor people meet their needs for small credit and other financial services. The informal and flexible services offered to low-income borrowers for meeting their modest consumption and livelihood needs have not only made microfinance movement grow at a rapid pace across the world, but in turn has also impacted the lives of millions of poor positively. This movement not only proved to be very successful, but has also emerged as the most popular form of microfinance in India.

Research methodology

Need for the study

Now-a-days, women are also playing a vital role in the economic development of the country by actively participating in various activities like managing the businesses, establishing business units, going abroad for the employment, indulging in research and developmental activities, contesting elections apart from managing household bearing children. There is no exception to rural women. They are bringing income with productive activities such as field working, running small and petty businesses etc. They have also proved that they can be better entrepreneurs and development managers in any kind of human development activities. Therefore, it is important to make rural women empowered in taking decisions to enable them to take part in economic development of the country. The empowerment of women also considered as an active process enabling women to realize their full identity and power in all spheres of life. In this regard government has introduced several schemes to empower rural women through Self-Help Groups and funding for these programmes through microfinance system, popularly known as Pavala Vaddi incentive. But how far the scheme is successful in meeting its objectives is a question mark? Hence it is needed to study the results of the scheme implemented by the government of Andhra Pradesh.

Objectives of the study

The following are the objectives set for the present study:

1. To understand the importance of Microfinance for women empowerment.
2. To evaluate the effectiveness of Pavala Vaddi strategy for DWCRA groups.
3. To find out the problems of Pavala Vaddi incentive scheme.
4. To suggest the suitable measures for effective utilization of the incentives offered to SHGs.

Sampling

A survey is being conducted in 89 village panchayats (1/10th of total number of village panchayats) of 13 mandals (1/3rd of total number of mandals) of Kadapa district were taken as sample for the study in order to arrive at meaningful results.

MICROFINANCE FOR WOMEN'S EMPOWERMENT

The programme has since come a long way from the pilot project of financing 500 SHGs across the country. It has proved its efficacy as a mainstream programme for banking with the poor, who mainly comprise the marginal farmers, landless labourers, artisans and craftsmen and others engaged in small businesses such as hawking and vending in the rural areas. The main advantages of the programme are timely repayment of loans to banks, reduction in transaction costs both to the poor and the banks, doorstep "saving and credit" facility for the poor and exploitation of the untapped business potential of the rural areas. The programme, which started as an outreach programme has not only aimed at promoting thrift and credit, but also contributed immensely towards the empowerment of the rural women.

Microfinance is emerging as a powerful instrument for poverty alleviation in the new economy. In India, microfinance scheme is dominated by Self-Help Groups (SHGs)–Bank Linkage programme, aimed at providing a cost-effective mechanism for providing financial services to the 'unreached poor'. The SHG programme has been successful in not only in meeting peculiar needs of the rural poor, but also in strengthening collective self-help capacities of the poor at the local level, leading to their empowerment.

Microfinance for the poor and women has gained expensive recognition as a strategy for poverty eradication and for economic empowerment. Finance for empowerment is about organizing people, particularly around credit and building capacities to manage money. The concentration is on making the poor to mobilize their own funds, building their capacities and empowering them. They will learn to manage money and rotate funds, builds women's capacities and confidence. Before 1990s, credit schemes for rural women were almost negligible. The concept of microfinance for women empowerment was both on the insistence by women-oriented studies that highlighted the discrimination and struggle of women in having the access to credit. The government measures have attempted to help the poor by implementing different poverty alleviation programmes but with little success. One among such measures is DWCRA. This programme is intended to develop the women and children of rural areas. The brief description, objectives, features, implementing agency and the incentives offered under this programme etc. are discussed below.

Introduction to DWCRA

In the year 1982, the Government of India launched Development of Women and Children in Rural Area

(DWCRA) as a sub-scheme of the Integrated Rural Development Programme (IRDP). It aims at involving the women in development activities by organizing them into groups. Besides, it focuses on social issues such as health, education, sanitation, nutrition and safe drinking water in rural areas. As the financial assistance to women was too marginal to enable them to cross the poverty line, it was felt, therefore, that a separate scheme should be drawn up, which would motivate women to come together and engage themselves in economically viable activities. With this in view, the Union Government in September 1982 launched DWCRA on a pilot basis as a sub-scheme of the IRDP.

Objectives of the DWCRA scheme

The main objectives of the scheme are:

1. Promotion of self-employment among rural women below the poverty line by providing them with skill training in vocations which are acceptable to them by encouraging productivity in their existing vocations and by introducing new activities wither to undertaking.
2. Organising the beneficiaries on the basis of group activity and promote economic and social self-reliance.
3. Generation of income for the rural poor by providing avenues for production of goods and services.
4. Promotion of production—enhancing programmes in rural areas.
5. Provision of facilities for care of children of working women.

Salient features

1. It is exclusively meant for women members of rural households, and to provide them avenues of income generation according to their skills, attitudes and local conditions.

2. For better inter-communication amongst women, group approach is adopted. The scheme envisages formation of groups of women within the age group of 18-65 years. From April 1991 onwards, each DWCRA group consist of 10-15 women.
3. Each group is given a one-time grant. The amount of grant was Rs. 15,000 but has since been raised to Rs. 25,000. The grant serves as a revolving fund to be used for marketing, childcare activities and purchase of few materials.
4. Provision exists for opening multi-purpose community centre for the groups to earn and for their economic and related activities.
5. Supportive services like mother and childcare, immunization, provision for working conveniences, adult education etc. are provided to rural women to improve their efficiency.
6. The group members, apart from deceiving benefits under DWCRA, are also entitled to loan and subsidy facilities under IRDP scheme.
7. The main activities undertaken by these groups under this scheme are bee-keeping and honey, fruit processing, sericulture, tailoring, basket weaving, match box, dress making, soap and candle making, knitting and weaving, poultry raising etc.
8. Each group selects one of its members as 'Group organiser' whose main function is to help in (*a*) Selection of an economic activity (*b*) Procurement of raw materials (*c*) marketing of finished products and (*d*) operation of bank account of the revolving fund.

Pavala Vaddi incentive to DWCRA (SHG) Groups

To encourage the women's groups further and also to achieve 100 per cent repayment, the State Government has introduced the PAVALA VADDI scheme, wherein the government is reimbursing to the members any interest paid by the SHGs over and above 3 per cent per annum. This has led to significant improvement in loan repayment. The table 11.1 describes the statistics of SHGs and Pavala Vaddi incentives.

Table 11.1

Particulars	Figures as on 31.01.2009
Number of SHGs	8,50,671
Number of members	1,01,82,151
Number of village organisations	35,525
Number of mandal samakhyas	1,098
Number of zilla samakhyas	22
Total savings in crores	1,962.50
Total corpus in crore	4,210.81

Source: www.rd.ap.gov.in

There are 1,01,82,151 members in 8,50,671 SHGs exclusively for women. A total of 35,525 village organizations (VOs), 1098 mandal samakhyas (MSs) and 22 zilla samakhyas have come into existence in 22 districts. As on today, the total savings and corpus of SHG members are Rs. 1962.50 crores and Rs. 4210.81 crores respectively.

Bank loans and Pavala Vaddi

During this financial year up to January 2009, Rs. 5934.52 crores of bank loans are given under Pavala Vaddi incentive as against annual target of Rs. 11,037 crores. Rs. 339.15 crores is given to SHG members as Pavala Vaddi Incentive.

Problems

In spite of many advantages, the Pavala Vaddi incentive scheme of DWCRA is suffering from few problems which are as under:

1. DWCRA is a group activity – obtaining co-ordination among all members is becoming difficult.

2. There is no provision for regular meetings to discuss credit needs, to establish priorities and to acquire the skills necessary to build and manage the institution.
3. If the products produced by DWCRA groups are not purchased by the government then marketing of that product is a major problem.
4. Many of the members are illiterates. They know only how to make their signature.
5. Still there is gender inequality.
6. Many of the DWCRA members doesn't have knowledge of the market and potential marketability for their products.
7. The local political leaders are influencing the sanction and allocation of credit.
8. Few of the government officials are not serious about the implementation of this programme.
9. Critical credit policies of Banks.
10. Many of the group leaders are collecting commission from the members for their services.

Suggestions

The following are the suggestions for achieving the targeted results of Microfinance for women empowerment.

1. The government needs to increase and expand their support in a liberal manner.
2. Political interference should be minimized
3. The eligibility criteria for sanctioning microfinance should also be based on the location or atmospheric conditions.
4. Training programmes should be conducted for women who borrowed Microfinance for the effective utilization of that amount.
5. More emphasis should also be given to educate the rural women.

6. Cost of Microfinance or interest rates of Microfinance should be still reduced to the groups which repay debt on time.
7. The training programmes should be conducted seriously.

Conclusion

Though there are few problems prevailed in the utilization of the funds by the members of SHGs, the objectives of this scheme are met considerably. But to ensure effective performance of the scheme, the government has to consider the above said suggestions.

12

Microfinance and Performance of Indira Kranthi Patham

An Overview

*Dr. P. Saritha
**Prof. P. Mohan Reddy
***Dr. C. Sivarami Reddy

ABSTRACT

Microfinance has been present in India in one form or another since the 1970s and is now widely accepted as an effective poverty alleviation strategy. The objectives of microfinance are, to achieve an understanding of key issues of microfinance; to obtain knowledge about the importance of designing the appropriate methodology and offer suitable products; to determine minimum requirements for microfinance practitioners and to provide basic knowledge about sustainability issues and performance measurements. There are three types of source of microfinance such as through formal, semi-formal and informal institutions. The specifically designed anti-poverty programmes for generation of both self-employment and wage-employment in rural areas have been redesigned and

* Assistant Professor, Department of MBA, YV University, Kadapa-516 003
** Associate Professor, Department of Commerce, Sri Venkateswara University, Tirupati-517 502, (A.P.)
*** Professor, Department of Commerce, Sri Venkateswara University, Tirupati-517 502, (A.P.)

restructured in 1999-2000 in order to enhance their efficacy or impact on the poor and improve their sustainability. They are, Swarna Jayanti Shahari Rozgar Yojana, Swarnajayanti Gram Swarozgar Yojana (SGSY), Jawahar Gram Samridhi Yojana (JGSY), Urban Self Employment Programme (USEP), Employment Assurance Scheme (EAS), Skill Training for Employment Promotion amongst Urban Poor (STEP-UP), Urban Wage Employment Programme (UWEP), Urban Community Development Network (UCDN), Urban Programme for Poverty Reduction amongst SCs & STs (UPPS), Indira Kranthi Patham (IKP), National Social Assistance Programme (NSAP), Indira Awaas Yojana (IAY) and the like.

The study is concentrated on Indira Kranthi Patham in Kadapa district, Andhra Pradesh and the performance of various programmes under Indira Kranti Patham. The main objective of Indira Kranthi Patham (IKP) is to eradicate the abject poverty in the rural areas of the state and to enable the poor in 22 rural districts of Andhra Pradesh to improve their livelihoods and quality of life. This objective is sought to be achieved through the active participation of the poor women and through their self-help groups and their federations. The project gives special focus to 29.86 lakh poorest of the poor families. Indira Kranthi Patham is implemented by the Society for Elimination of Rural Poverty (SERP), an autonomous society registered under Public Societies Act. The management of the society is vested with a seven member Executive Council (EC). To encourage the women's groups further and also to achieve 100 per cent repayment, the state government have introduced the PAVALA VADDI scheme from 2004-05 onwards. The CIF provides resources to the poor communities for use as means to improve their livelihoods. Food security intervention addresses this hunger gap in rural communities. Under land purchase component productive and ready to use land with assured irrigation facility is being given to the poorest of the poor households in the rural areas. The marketing interventions in IKP have registered a significant increase in this financial year with paddy procurement under minimum support price.

Introduction

Microfinance has been present in India in one form or another since the 1970s and is now widely accepted as an effective poverty alleviation strategy. Microfinance is one sector which is not clearly or particularly defined However, there have many efforts to define. Once such effort was done by a taskforce set up by the RBI where they said that it is the provision of financial services for the poor. It is a process of activating and involving societies in nation buildings on the theme of self and mutual help with the aim of endowing them with resources, confidence and sustainable livelihood lifestyles. These financial services including savings, credit, insurance and the like. Over the last five years, the microfinance industry has achieved significant growth in part due to the participation of commercial banks. Despite this growth, the poverty situation in India continuous to be challenging. Microfinance is a powerful poverty-fighting tool. Microfinance helps people to escape poverty by giving them collateral-free loans and other financial services to support income-generating businesses. We support microfinance programs that enable the poor, mostly women, to lift themselves out of poverty and make better lives for their families. As each loan is repaid, the money is redistributed as loans to others, thereby multiplying its impact.

Objectives of microfinance

- To achieve an understanding of key issues of microfinance.
- To obtain knowledge about the importance of designing the appropriate methodology and offer suitable products.
- To determine minimum requirements for microfinance practitioners
- To provide basic knowledge about sustainability issues and performance measurements.

Key aspects of microfinance

- Microfinance would get recognized and organized as an industry in India.
- The combined outreach of microfinance institutions and banks would have increased to 25 per cent of India's poor.
- Commercial banks and MFIs will come together as partners and the government will have worked constructively with NGOs to solve many of the problems faced by microfinance sector.
- Savings services would be available for all poor clients through both banks and microfinance institutions.
- The regional disparities in microfinance outreach would get addressed through both the bank linkage programme as also microfinance institutions.

Types of source of microfinance

Institutional microfinance includes microfinance services provided by both formal and semi-formal institutions. Microfinance institutions are institutions whose major business is the provision of microfinance scarce. There are three types of source of microfinance

1. Formal Institutions - Rural banks and corporate banks
2. Semi-formal Institutions - Non-government organizations
3. Informal Sources - Moneylenders and shopkeepers.

Programmes of microfinance and poverty alleviation in A.P.

The specifically designed anti-poverty programmes for generation of both self-employment and wage-employment in rural areas have been redesigned and restructured in

1999-2000 in order to enhance their efficacy or impact on the poor and improve their sustainability. They are:

- Swarna Jayanti Shahari Rozgar Yojana
- Swarnajayanti Gram Swarozgar Yojana (SGSY)
- Jawahar Gram Samridhi Yojana (JGSY)
- Urban Self Employment Programme (USEP)
- Employment Assurance Scheme (EAS)
- Skill Training for Employment Promotion amongst Urban Poor (STEP-UP)
- Urban Wage Employment Programme (UWEP)
- Urban Community Development Network (UCDN)
- Urban Programme for Poverty Reduction amongst SCs & STs (UPPS)
- Indira Kranthi Patham (IKP)
- National Social Assistance Programme (NSAP)
- Indira Awaas Yojana (IAY)

Aim of the study

The study is concentrated on Indira Kranthi Patham in Kadapa district, Andhra Pradesh and the performance of various programmes under Indira Kranti Patham.

Period of the study

The study period consists of from 2001-02 to 2007-08.

Objectives of Indira Kranthi Patham

This is a statewide, community demand driven rural poverty alleviation project aiming to cover all rural poor households in the state, with a special focus on 29.86 lakh poorer households. The main objective of Indira Kranthi Patham (IKP) is to eradicate the abject poverty in the rural areas of the state and to enable the poor in 22 rural districts of Andhra Pradesh to improve their livelihoods and quality of life. This objective is sought to be achieved through the active participation of the poor women and through their self-help groups and their federations. The project gives special focus to 29.86 lakh poorest of the poor families.

The SHG movements has taken firm roots in the state of Andhra Pradesh from 1991 onwards. The World Bank financed Andhra Pradesh districts poverty initiatives project (APDPIP) called Andhra Pradesh Rural Poverty Reduction Project (APRPRP) was introduced in the remaining 548 mandals of 16 rural districts of Andhra Pradesh in 2003.

Project implementation

Indira Kranthi Patham is implemented by the Society for Elimination of Rural Poverty (SERP), an autonomous society registered under Public Societies Act. The management of the society is vested with a seven member Executive Council (EC). The Honb'le Chief Minister is the president of the general body of the society and the Honb'le Minister for Rural Development is vice-president of the general body and the president of the executive council. The ex-officio members of the EC are principal secretary (Department of Rural Development), Commissioner (Rural Development), Commissioner (Tribal Welfare) and chief executive officer of the society.

At the state level, the project is managed by a State Project Management Unit (SPMU), comprising CEO and additional CEO assisted by regional project directors and other functional specialists in institution building, training, gender, microfinance, communications, livelihoods promotion, marketing, monitoring and learning.

At the district level, there is a District Project Management Unit (DPMU) headed by a Project Director (PD), assisted by functional specialists. The activities of District Rural Development Agency (DRDA) and IKP were integrated through a government order and the PD, IKP is also the PD, DRDA. Specialists at both SPMU and DPMU are drawn from government, NGOs and open market. At the sub-district level, there is one area coordinator for 4 to 6 mandals to concentrate on institution and capacity-building of the poor.

At the grassroots level, the community based organizations—mandal samakhyas and village organizations—implement various project components. The village organization which is a federation of all SHGs in a village is registered as a cooperative society under the Mutually Aided Cooperative Societies Act and the mandal samkhya is registered as a federation of coopereatives.

PROGRESS OF INDIRA KRANTI PATHAM

Institutional and human-capacity building

The institution and human capacity building facilitates the formation and strengthening of self-managed institutions of the poor and helps in building social and human capital. There were a total of 3,73,044 SHGs as on 2000-01. The number of groups added during the last seven years is given in Table 12.1.

Table 12.1

Year	No. of groups formed
2001-02	50,322
2002-03	27,882
2003-04	59,839
2004-05	72,667
2005-06	44,758
2006-07	59,746
2007-08	2,71,937
Total	**2269.49**

However, as the vast majority of the rural poor are already organized into SHGs, growth of new SHGs is expected to be moderate in the coming years. There were a total of 50,65,539 SHGs members as on 2001-02. The number of members during the last seven years is given in Table 12.2.

The SHG movement in Andhra Pradesh has taken deep roots in all districts of Andhra Pradesh, and as a result there are 87,52,540 SHG members in 6,99,056 SHGs organized into 33,907 Village Organizations(VOs) and 1,083 Mandal Samakhyas. In addition, there are 126 Mandal Vikalangula Sangams, 17 Chenchu Mandal Samakhyas and 15 Fisher Men Mandal Samakhyas in the state. District Samakhyas (DS) have come into existence in all the 22 districts. More than 90 per cent of the poorest of the poor and poor SC and ST families in AP. are organized into SHGs.

Table 12.2

Year	No. of members enrolled
2001-02	5,79,470
2002-03	4,10,272
2003-04	7,00,820
2004-05	8,18,229
2005-06	4,02,911
2006-07	6,46,522
2007-08	2,85,120
Total	**2,269.49**

Financial support to SHGs through SHG-Bank Linkages

The SHG-Bank Linkage is a great success story in A.P. There are 4,124 rural bank branches belonging to 18 Commercial Banks and 5 Regional Rural Banks participating in the SHG bank linkage programme. Bank lending to SHGs was Rs 197.70 crores in 2001-02 and the progress went up to touch Rs 752.90 crores in 2003-04. Due to Pavala Vaddi incentive introduced in 2004-05, Bank Linkages have taken a dramatic upward movement after 2004-05. Year-wise bank linkages during the last six years are given in table 12.3.

Compare to an amount of Rs. 1404.70 crores during 3 year period from 2001-02 to 2003-04, the bank loans to the SHGs have increased to Rs. 6082.97 crores during the 3 year period from 2004-05 to 2006-07. This is the phenomenal increase of around 333 per cent over the last 3 year period. The SHGs in A.P. are able to secure Rs. 84,000 per SHG which is 70 per cent higher than the rest of India figure which stands at Rs. 48,000. Due to the strong support given by the state government, the banks have agreed to finance all genuine financial needs of the poor women enrolled in SHGs. This has led to the Total Financial Inclusive (TFI) concept in the year 2006-07 where, in 304 villages, the banks financed SHGs for all their needs including retiring high cost debts, income generation needs and social needs. Each SHG depending on their requirements was provided financial support up to Rs. 5 lakhs. This is a very successful intervention and in 2007-08, 4000 villages are going to be covered under total financial inclusion. In the next 3 years, all villages will be covered under total financial inclusion. The target for bank loans during 2007-08 is Rs. 6527.00.

Table 12.3

Year	No. of groups	Rs. in crores
2001-02	88,575	197.70
2002-03	1,65,429	454.10
2003-04	2,31,336	752.90
2004-05	2,61,254	1017.70
2005-06	2,88,711	2001.40
2006-07	3,66,489	3063.87
2007-08	71,937	6527.00
Total	**14,01,794**	**7487.67**

Financial access and Pavala Vaddi initiative

To encourage the women's groups further and also to achieve 100 per cent repayment, the state government have introduced the Pavala Vaddi scheme from 2004-05 onwards.

Under this initiative, the government ensures that the interest burden to the SHG members on bank loans does not exceed 3 per cent per annum. The details are given in table 12.4. The target for Pavala Vaddi incentive during 2007-08 alone is Rs. 100.0 crores and a sum of Rs. 76.58 crores to SHG members under this scheme has been disbursed. Pavala Vaddi incentive has inculcated a habit of prompt repayment of bank loans by SHG members with the result that the average loan recovery is now 98.7 per cent in the state, with 100 per cent recovery in most of the cases.

Table 12.4

Year	No. of groups	Rs. in crores
2004-05	2,00,458	52.69
2005-06	2,74,706	50.00
2006-07	2,01,400	102.69
2007-08	2,95,698	198.97
Total	**2,269.49**	**2,269.49**

Pavala Vaddi incentive has inculcated a habit of prompt repayment of bank loans by SHG members with the result that the average loan recovery is now 98.7 per cent in the state, with 100 per cent recovery in most of the cases.

Community investment fund (CIF)

The CIF provides resources to the poor communities for use as means to improve their livelihoods. This component supports the poor in prioritizing livelihood needs by investments in sub-projects proposed and implemented by themselves or through their Community Based Organisations (CBOs). CIF is a one time grant to the Mandal Samakhyas by IKP. However, this CIF is rotated among SHG members again and again to increase their investment in income-generating activities. The total CIF expenditure upto 2003-04 was Rs. 232.49 crores. The year-wise details of CIF expenditure up to 2007-08 are given in table 12.5.

Table 12.5

Year	Rs. in crores
2001-02	4.01
2002-03	47.73
2003-04	180.75
2004-05	217.78
2005-06	177.91
2006-07	142.00
2007-08	40.00
Total	**597.69**

Food security

In the lean agricultural season, many of the rural poor have barely one square meal a day. Food security intervention addresses this hunger gap in rural communities. Through this scheme, the VOs encourage SHG members to draw their full PDS quota and ensure that the members utilize this opportunity. For the balance, the VOs estimate the bulk requirement of SHG members for rice and other essential commodities, negotiate and buy better quality commodities from the open market and sell to their members at a price lower than the retail outlets. The amount is repaid in instalments. Food security initiative has taken off after 2004-05. Under this initiative, 12,91,771 families were covered between 2004-05 and 2007-08. The details of the beneficiary families covered by food security are given in table 12.6.

Table 12.6 : Beneficiaries of food security initiative

S. No.	Item	Number
1.	No. of districts covered	22
2.	No. of VOs covered	18,495
3.	No. of SHGs covered	1,80,288
4.	Number of families covered	15,59,433

Land purchase

Under this component productive and ready to use land with assured irrigation facility is being given to the poorest of the poor households in the rural areas. As on 2008, an extent of 4455.34 acres of land was purchased and handed over to 4808 poor families. The cost of this land is Rs. 29.11 crores. This is a completely new initiative introduced after 2004-05 and the details of year-wise land purchased and value of the land are given in table 12.7.

Table 12.7

Year	No. of acres	Rs. in crores
2004-05	597.97	2.00
2005-06	2376.8	14.97
2006-07	1168.2	9.25
2007-08	4455.34	29.11
Total	**2269.49**	**2269.49**

Community managed sustainable agriculture

The main objective of the Community Managed Sustainable Agriculture (CMSA) is to sustain agriculture based livelihoods, increasing net incomes by reducing cost of cultivation with adoption of practices involving low or no expenditure with special focus on small and marginal farmers in general and women farmers in particular. Outreach of CMSA is gaining momentum. This program began in the year 2005-06 in 450 villages in 10,000 ha and it spread to 18 districts, 1832 villages and in 3 lakh ha and 2 lakh farmers this year.

Collective marketing

The marketing interventions in IKP have registered a significant increase in this financial year with Paddy procurement under Minimum Support price. Collective Marketing activity was in a nascent stage up to 2003-04. The details of collective marketing activity up to 2007-08 are shown in table 12.8.

Table 12.8

Year	Quintals	Rs. in crores
2001-02	5,027	0.73
2002-03	21,440	2.27
2003-04	43,748	6.09
2004-05	1,80,036	16.00
2005-06	25,08,745	141.90
2006-07	18,03,595	127.02
2007-08	45,00,000	325.00
Total	**2269.49**	**2269.49**

Pensions

The amount distributed for Pensions was very moderate up to 2003-04. The total expenditure under pensions between 2001-02 and 2007-08 are given in table 12.9.

Table 12.9

Year	No. of pensions	Rs. in crores
2001-02	13,19,400	124.12
2002-03	15,19,400	137.70
2003-04	15,19,400	137.70
2004-05	15,19,400	147.97
2005-06	16,69,400	202.59
2006-07	29,04,528	709.97
2007-08	36,78,325	809.44
Total	**2269.49**	**2269.49**

Summing up

Traditionally, microfinance has focused on providing very small loans (micro-credit) to the poor to help them engage in productive activities. But overtime microfinance has come to include a broader range of services and are come to recognize that the poor require a variety of financial services to meet their daily needs including a safe place to save, payment and money transfer services, and insurance. All of these financial services can help poor people to smooth consumption flows, invest in productive activities, boost their income and reduce their vulnerability to all types of risks and ultimately allow them to plan for their own futures. Unfortunately, only a small proportion of people in developing countries who could make use of these services currently have access.

Most poor people manage to mobilize resources to develop their enterprises and their dwellings slowly overtime. Financial services could enable the poor to leverage their initiative, accelerating the process of building incomes, assets and economic security. Acceleration of economic growth, with a focus on sectors which are employment-intensive, facilitates the removal of poverty in the long run. However, this strategy needs to be complemented with a focus laid on provision of basic services for improving the quality of life of the people and direct state intervention in the form of targeted anti-poverty programmes. Anti-poverty programmes supplement the growth effort and protect the poor from destitution, sharp fluctuations in employment and incomes and social insecurity.

REFERENCES

1. "Note on Self-Employment Schemes in Kadapa District," DRDA, Kadapa.
2. K.G. Kamarkar, *Rural Credit and Self-Help-Groups' Microfinance Needs and Concepts in India*, Sage Publications, New Delhi, 1999.
3. Francin R. Frankel, *India Political Economy 1947-2004*, Oxford University Press, Bombay, 1998.
4. http://www. grdc.org/icm
5. Agnihotri, S.P., *National Employment Programmes in India*, Chough, Allahabad, 1992.
6. V. Nirmala, K. Shambhat and P. Bhuvaneswari, "SHGs Cohesiveness in DWCRA Groups; An Application of Sociometric Approach", *Kurukshetra*, Vol. XLIII, No. 8 and 9, May-June, 1995.

13

Microfinance: A Boon for the Empowerment of Women in India

*Dr. G. Vijaya Bharathi
**Mr. P. Harinatha Reddy
***Kum. V. Lakshmi Thulasi

ABSTRACT

Microfinance for the poor and women has received extensive recognition as a strategy for poverty reduction and for economic empowerment. Increasingly in the last five years, there is questioning of whether micro-credit is most effective approach to economic empowerment of poorest and, among them, women in particular. Development practitioners in India and developing countries often argue that the exaggerated focus on microfinance as a solution for the poor has led to neglect by the state and public institutions in addressing employment and livelihood needs of the poor. Credit for empowerment is about organizing people, particularly around credit and building capacities to manage money. The focus is on getting the poor to mobilize their own funds, building their capacities and empowering them to leverage external credit. Perception of

* Assistant Professor, Department of Commerce, YV University, Kadapa-516 003

** Research Scholar, Department of Commerce, Sri Venkateswara University, Tirupati-517 502, A.P.

*** Research Scholar, Department of Commerce, Sri Venkateswara University, Tirupati-517 502, A.P.

women is that learning to manage money and rotate funds builds women's capacities and confidence to intervene in local governance beyond the limited goals of ensuring access to credit. The term microfinance is of recent origin and is commonly used in addressing issues related to poverty alleviation, financial support to micro-entrepreneurs, gender development and the like. There is, however, no statutory definition of microfinance.

Savings and credit programmes should be designed in a way not to exclude women from participating. Additionally, there is a need to examine the impact of structural adjustment policies on men and women at the family level as well as within various sub-sectors of the labour market and within the small enterprise sector itself. In general terms, in order to facilitate the participation of women in micro- and small-enterprise, donors should (i) encourage micro-enterprise programmes to develop specific strategies for recruiting women as clients from within their existing target groups, (ii) encourage micro-enterprise programmes to expand their target groups to include the sizes and types of enterprise activities in which women engage and/or experiment with assistance strategies, business and technical assistance needs of these types of enterprises and (iii) consider expanding support to a broader range of organisations, especially poverty-focused organisations active in rural areas. Microfinance activities can give them a means to climb out of poverty. Microfinance could be a solution to help them to extend their horizon and offer them social recognition and empowerment. Financial empowerment has, in many cases, helped women acquire more self-esteem, more respect within their families, and has even linked to decreases in domestic violence. Empowered women also have a positive impact on their communities, and are considered to be more responsive to the long-term needs of their households than men. The key issue for successful microfinance program focused on women should consider them in a broader context, as a family nucleus, that is vital for societal improvement and progress. Following this idea, microfinance programmes should provide women with specific adapted products through appropriate methodologies, which can offer competitiveness to their business but also well being to them and their families.

Introduction

All over the world, the significant of women entry into the workforce over the past three decades has produced profound transformations in the organisation of families, society, the economy, and urban life. Since the late 1950s, women's economic activities have been steadily increasing. Women have always actively participated in their local economies. In Africa, for example, women produce 80 per cent of the food and in Asia 60 per cent and in Latin America 40 per cent. In many cases, women not only produce the food but market it as well, which gives them a well-developed knowledge of local markets and customers.

In spite of the remarkable importance of women's participation, their jobs have been considered as an "extra income" to family survival or simply to improve its living conditions. Moreover, micro-enterprises owned by women have been considered as a way to meet primary needs instead of a profitable source of income. Unfortunately, labour markets have followed this perception and have offered less favorable conditions to women. Women workers consistently earn less than their male partners do. Women have had to fight against an adverse environment, which traditionally had been minimising and exploiting their capacities. As a consequence of this reality, in some cases, women are just satisfied with the non-financial benefits, such as the psychological satisfaction of "social contact".

Concept and definitions of microfinance

The term microfinance is of recent origin and is commonly used in addressing issues related to poverty alleviation, financial support to micro-entrepreneurs, gender development and the like. There is, however, no statutory definition of microfinance. The taskforce on Supportitative Policy and Regulatory Framework for Microfinance has defined microfinance as "Provision of thrift, credit and other financial services and products of very small amounts to the poor in rural, semi-urban or urban areas for enabling them to raise their income levels and improve living standards". The term "Micro" literally means "small". But the taskforce has not defined any amount. However as per Micro Credit Special Cell of the Reserve Bank of India, the borrowal amounts upto the limit of Rs. 25,000 could be considered as micro-credit products and this amount could be gradually increased up to Rs. 40,000 over a period of time.

The term microfinance, sometimes is used interchangeably with the term micro-credit. However while micro-credit refers to purveyance of loans in small quantities, the term microfinance has a broader meaning covering in its ambit other financial services like saving, insurance and the like as well. The mantra "Microfinance" is banking through groups. The essential features of the approach are to provide financial services through the groups of individuals, formed either in joint liability or co-obligation mode.

Dimensions of microfinance

The dimensions of the microfinance approach are:

- Savings/Thrift precedes credit
- Credit is linked with savings/thrift
- Absence of subsidies
- Group plays an important role in credit appraisal, monitoring and recovery.

Women and microfinance

Although men, as well as women, face difficulties in establishing an additional enterprise, women have barriers to overcome. Among them are negative socio-cultural attitudes, legal barriers, practical external barriers, lack of education and personal difficulties. In spite of this, for women and especially for poor women, micro-entreprise ownership has emerged as a strategy for economical survival. One of the most essential factors contributing to success in micro-entrepreneurship is access to capital and financial services. For various reasons, women have had less access to these services than men.

In this context, credit for micro-enterprise development has been a crucial issue over the past two decades. Research has shown that investing in women offers the most effective means to improve health, nutrition, hygiene, and educational standards for families and consequently for the whole of society. Thus, a special support for women in both financial and non-financial services is necessary. Regarding limited access to financial services, women depend largely on their own limited cash resources or, in some cases, loans from extended family members for investment capital. Smaller amounts of investment capital effectively limit women to a narrow range of low-return activities which require minimal capital outlays, few tools and equipment and rely on farm produce or inexpensive raw materials. In general, women need access to small loans, innovative forms of collateral, frequent repayment schedules more appropriate to the cash flows of their enterprises, simpler application procedures and improved access to saving accounts.

Elements for women failure in business

Surveys have shown that many elements contribute to make it more difficult for women in small businesses to make a profit. These elements are:

- Lack of knowledge of the market and potential profitability, thus making the choice of business difficult.
- Inadequate bookkeeping.
- Employment of too many relatives which increases social pressure to share benefits.
- Setting prices arbitrarily.
- Lack of capital.
- High interest rates.

- Inventory and inflation accounting is never undertaken.
- Credit policies that can gradually run their business.

WOMEN'S EMPOWERMENT AND MICROFINANCE: DIFFERENT PARADIGMS

Concern with women's access to credit and assumptions about contributions to women's empowerment are not new. From the early 1970s women's movements in a number of countries became increasingly interested in the degree to which women were able to access poverty-focused credit programmes and credit cooperatives. In India organizations like Self-Employed Women's Association (SEWA) among others with origins and affiliations in the Indian labour and women's movements identified credit as a major constraint in their work with informal sector women workers.

The problem of women's access to credit was given particular emphasis at the first International Women's Conference in Mexico in 1975 as part of the emerging awareness of the importance of women's productive role both for national economies, and for women's rights. This led to the setting up of the Women's World Banking network and production of manuals for women's credit provision. Other women's organizations world-wide set up credit and savings components both as a way of increasing women's incomes and bringing women together to address wider gender issues. From the mid-1980s there was a mushrooming of donor, government and NGO-sponsored credit programmes in the wake of the 1985 Nairobi women's conference (Mayoux, 1995a).

The 1980s and 1990s also saw development and rapid expansion of large minimalist poverty-targeted microfinance institutions and networks like Grameen Bank and ACCION among others. In these organizations and others evidence of significantly higher female repayment rates led to increasing emphasis on targeting women as an efficiency strategy to increase credit recovery. A number of donors also saw female-targeted financially-sustainable microfinance as a means of marrying internal demands for increased efficiency because of declining budgets with demands of the increasingly vocal gender lobbies.

The trend was further reinforced by the Micro Credit Summit Campaign starting in 1997 which had 'reaching and empowering women' as its second key goal after poverty reduction (RESULTS, 1997). Microfinance for women has recently been seen as a key strategy in meeting not only Millennium Goal 3 on gender equality, but also poverty reduction, health, HIV/AIDS and other goals.

Feminist Empowerment Paradigm

The feminist empowerment paradigm did not originate as a Northern imposition, but is firmly rooted in the development of some of the earliest microfinance programmes in the South, including SEWA in India. It currently underlies the gender policies of many NGOs and the perspectives of some of the consultants and researchers looking at gender impact of microfinance programmes. Here the underlying concerns are gender equality and women's human rights. Women's empowerment is seen as an integral and inseparable part of a wider process of social transformation. The main target group is poor women and women capable of providing alternative female role models for change. Increasing attention has also been paid to men's role in challenging gender inequality.

Microfinance is promoted as an entry point in the context of a wider strategy for women's economic and socio-political empowerment which focuses on gender awareness and feminist organization. As developed by Chen in her proposals for a sub-sector approach to micro-credit, based partly on SEWA's strategy and promoted by UNIFEM, microfinance must be:

- Part of a sectoral strategy for change which identifies opportunities, constraints and bottlenecks within industries which if addressed can raise returns and prospects for large numbers of women. Possible strategies include linking women to existing services and infrastructure, developing new technology such as labour-saving food processing, building information networks, shifting to new markets, policy level changes to overcome legislative barriers and unionization.

- Based on participatory principles to build up incremental knowledge of industries and enable women to develop their strategies for change (Chen, 1996). Economic empowerment is however defined in more than individualist terms to include issues such as property rights, changes in intra-household relations and transformation of the macro-economic context. Many organisations go further than interventions at the industry level to include gender-specific strategies for social and political empowerment. Some programmes have developed very effective means for integrating gender awareness into programmes and for organizing women and men to challenge and change gender discrimination.

Poverty Reduction Paradigm

The poverty alleviation paradigm underlies many NGO integrated poverty-targeted community development programmes. Poverty alleviation here is defined in broader terms than market incomes to encompass increasing capacities and choices and decreasing the vulnerability of the poor people. The main focus of programmes as a whole is on developing sustainable livelihoods, community development and social service provision like literacy, health care and infrastructure development. There is not only a concern with reaching the poor, but also the poorest. Policy debates have focused particularly on the importance of small savings and loan provision for consumption as well as production, group formation and the possible justification for some level of subsidy for programmes working with particular client groups or in particular contexts. Some programmes have developed effective methodologies for poverty targeting and/or operating in remote areas. Such strategies have recently become a focus of interest from some donors and also the Micro Credit Summit Campaign.

Here gender lobbies have argued for targeting women because of higher levels of female poverty and women's responsibility for household well-being. However, although gender inequality is recognized as an issue, the focus is on assistance to households and there is a tendency to see gender issues as cultural and hence not subject to outside intervention. Although term 'empowerment' is frequently used in general terms, often synonymous with a multi-dimensional definition of poverty alleviation, the term 'women's empowerment' is often considered best avoided as being too controversial and political. The assumption is that increasing women's access to microfinance will enable women to make a greater contribution to household income and this, together with other interventions to increase household well-being, will translate into improved well-being for women and enable women to bring about wider changes in gender inequality.

Financial Sustainability Paradigm

The financial self-sustainability paradigm underlies the models of microfinance promoted since the mid-1990s by most donor agencies and the Best Practice guidelines promoted in publications by USAID, World Bank, UNDP and CGAP. The ultimate aim is on the programmes which are profitable and fully self-supporting in competition with other private sector banking institutions and able to raise funds from international financial markets rather than relying on funds from development agencies. The main target group, despite claims to reach the poorest, is the 'bankable poor': small entrepreneurs and farmers. This emphasis on financial sustainability is seen as necessary to create institutions which reach significant numbers of poor people in the context of declining aid budgets and opposition to welfare and redistribution in macro-economic policy.

Policy discussions have focused particularly on setting up of interest rates to cover costs, separation of microfinance from other interventions to enable separate accounting and programme expansion to increase outreach and economies of scale, reduction of transaction costs and ways of using groups to decrease costs of delivery. Recent guidelines for CGAP funding and best practice focus on production of a 'financial sustainability index' which charts progress of programmes in covering costs from incomes. Within this paradigm gender lobbies have been able to argue for targeting women on the grounds of high female repayment rates and the need to stimulate women's economic activity as a hitherto underutilized resource for economic growth.

These paradigms do not correspond systematically to any one organisational model of microfinance. Microfinance providers with the same organisational form, e.g. village bank, Grameen model or cooperative model may have very different gender policies and/or emphases and strategies for poverty alleviation. The three paradigms represent different 'discourses' each with its own relatively consistent internal logic in relating aims to policies, based on different underlying understandings of development. They are not only different, but often seen as 'incompatible discourses' in uneasy tension and with continually contested degrees of dominance. In many programmes and donor agencies there is considerable disagreement, lack of communication and/or personal animosity and promoted by different stakeholders within organisations between staff involved in microfinance, staff concerned with human development gender lobbies.

MICROFINANCE INSTRUMENT FOR WOMEN'S EMPOWERMENT

Microfinance for the poor and women has received extensive recognition as a strategy for poverty reduction and for economic empowerment. Increasingly in the last five years, there is questioning of whether micro-credit is most effective approach to economic empowerment of poorest and, among them, women in particular. Development practitioners in India and developing countries often argue that the exaggerated focus on microfinance as a solution for the poor has led to neglect by the state and public institutions in addressing employment and livelihood needs of the poor.

Credit for empowerment is about organizing people, particularly around credit and building capacities to manage money. The focus is on getting the poor to mobilize their own funds, building their capacities and empowering them to leverage external credit. Perception of women is that learning to manage money and rotate funds builds women's capacities and confidence to intervene in local governance beyond the limited goals of ensuring access to credit. Further, it combines the goals of financial sustainability with that of creating community owned institutions.

Before 1990s, credit schemes for rural women were almost negligible. The concept of women's credit was born on the insistence by women-oriented studies that highlighted the discrimination and struggle of women in having the access of credit. However, there is a perceptible gap in financing genuine credit needs of the poor especially women in the rural sector. There are certain misconception about the poor people that they need loan at subsidized rate of interest on soft terms, they lack education, skill, capacity to save, credit worthiness and therefore are not bankable. Nevertheless, the experience of several SHGs reveal that rural poor are actually efficient managers of credit and finance.

The government measures have attempted to help the poor by implementing different poverty alleviation programmes but with little success. Since most of them are target based involving lengthy procedures for loan disbursement, high transaction costs, and lack of supervision and monitoring. Since the credit requirements of the rural poor cannot be adopted on project lending approach as it is in the case of organized sector, there emerged the need for an informal credit supply through SHGs. The rural poor with the assistance from NGOs have demonstrated their potential for self help to secure economic and financial strength. Various case studies show that there is a positive correlation between credit availability and women's empowerment.

Steps to increase women's participation in microfinance activities

Both governments and donors should explore ways of developing innovative credit programmes using intermediary channels or institutions closer to the target groups such as co-operatives, women's group associations and other grassroots organisations. Savings and credit programmes should be designed in a way not to exclude women from participating. Additionally, there is a need to examine the impact of structural adjustment policies on men and women at the family level as well as within various sub-sectors of the labour market and within the small enterprise sector itself. In general terms, in order to facilitate the participation of women in micro- and small-enterprise, donors should:

- Encourage micro-enterprise programmes to develop specific strategies for recruiting women as clients from within their existing target groups.
- Encourage micro-enterprise programmes to expand their target groups to include the sizes and types of enterprise activities in which women engage and/or experiment with assistance strategies, business and technical assistance needs of these types of enterprises.
- Consider expanding support to a broader range of organisations, especially poverty-focused organisations active in rural areas. Support for these organisations should include technical assistance and training in programme planning, management and in developing teams of female staff to assist clients in business planning and management.

Conclusions

Traditionally women have been marginalised. A high percentage of women are among the poorest of the poor. Microfinance activities can give them a means to climb out of poverty. Microfinance could be a solution to help them to extend their horizon and offer them social recognition and empowerment. Financial empowerment has, in many cases, helped women acquire more self-esteem, more respect within their families, and has even linked to decreases in domestic violence. Empowered women also have a positive impact on their communities, and are considered to be more responsive to the long-term needs of their households than men. The key issue for successful microfinance program focused on women should consider them in a broader context, as a family nucleus, that is vital for societal improvement and progress. Following this idea, microfinance programmes should provide women with specific adapted products through appropriate methodologies, which can offer competitiveness to their business but also well being to them and their families.

REFERENCES

1. www.fwa.org/community/microfinance.htm
2. http://www.un.org.in/iawg/icecd/section1.htm
3. Small Enterprise Development, An International Journal Vol. 9 No. 3, September 98, 1998, p. 72.
4. Balancing the double day: Women as managers of micro enterprises, Eliana Restrepo Chebairy Rebecca Reichmann, ACCION Internacional, Monograph Series No. 10, Colombia, 1995, p. 84.

14

Microfinance through Self-Help Groups

Status and Emerging Challenges

*Dr. Smt. P. Subbalakshumma
**Dr. P. Saritha

Introduction

Microfinance is emerging as a powerful instrument for poverty alleviation in the new economy. In India, microfinance scene is dominated by Self-Help Groups (SHGs)–Bank Linkage Programme, aimed at providing a cost-effective mechanism for providing financial services to the "unreached poor". Based on the philosophy of peer pressure and group savings as collateral substitute, the SHG programme has been successful in not only in meeting peculiar needs of the rural poor, but also in strengthening collective self-help capacities of the poor at the local level, leading to their empowerment. Microfinance is about provision of thrift, credit and other financial services and products of very small amounts to the poor in rural, semi-urban or urban areas for enabling them to raise their income levels and to improve their living standards (NABARD, 1999). Banks in India have been giving small loans and have been

* Associate Professor, Department of Commerce, SKR & SKR GDC Women, Kadapa-516 003
** Assistant Professor, Department of MBA, Y.V. University, Kadapa-516 003

accepting small deposits. It is reported that about 55 per cent of all loans given by all scheduled commercial banks in India are small loans, i.e. less than Rs. 25,000 as on March 2004.

Microfinance has certain design principles:

- These design principles are: small saving or thrift by poor is possible if collected at doorsteps;
- poor people need small collateral free loans with frequency instead of large loans at a time;
- non-rigidity of end use is preferred by poor people over rigid end use of small loans repayment to match with existing family cash flow instead of individual cash flow or project cash flow;
- rate of interest is not crucial relative to hassle free, timely, adequate and continued credit facility;
- relatively small repayment periods are preferred, e.g. weekly, fortnightly, monthly, instead of half-yearly, yearly, etc. intensive supervision is required for microfinance operations;
- women are better customers relative to men; and
- group method of lending is more successful relative to individual lending.

Studies report that poor rural households require about Rs. 6,000 per annum and a poor urban household requires on an average about Rs. 9,000 per annum. The total credit requirement of rural and urban poor households in India works out to be about Rs. 49,500 crores. The estimates, however, have ranged from Rs. 30,000 crore to Rs. 200,000 crore and shows the magnitude of business that is involved if all poor households are to be reached by formal financial institutions. The current supply figures pertaining to SHG-Bank linkage programme are in the range of Rs 180 billion as on March 2007.

SELF-HELP GROUPS AND THEIR LINKAGE WITH BANKS

One of the successful ways through which microfinance services are being provided to poor people is through Self-

Help Groups. It all started with experiments of some non-government organizations (NGOs) working in south India during early 1980s and has now come to be known as Self-Help Group approach to microfinance. With intervention of RBI, National Bank for Agriculture and Rural Development (NABARD), Small Industries Development Bank of India (SIDBI), Rashtriya Mahila Kosh (RMK) and other organisations, Self-Help Group-bank linkage has become a supplementary channel for providing financial services from formal financial institutions to poor people. Under this linkage arrangement, SHGs are assessed by bank for bank credit after about six months of their functioning. If SHGs are found functioning well, then, bank credit is sanctioned up to four times the savings of the SHG.

The Self-Help Groups (SHGs) are essentially informal voluntary associations of people formed to attain a collective goal. People who are homogeneous with respect to social background, heritage, caste or traditional occupations come together for a common cause to raise and manage their collective savings for the benefit of all the group members. Usually, the focus is on poor and that too on women.

The process through which selected people, usually poor, representing a specific economic strata of society, with some specific identity (of caste, occupation, origin, etc.) are encouraged to form small homogeneous groups for the purpose of participating in development activities, i.e. savings, credit, income generation etc. is called 'Group Formation' or 'Group Promotion' or 'Group Evolution'.

The SHGs can be formed for any common cause or development activity. Normally it is found that initially though the groups are formed for a specific activity, gradually they diversify and take up more than one development activity in the area. SHGs practicing saving and credit along with other activities have been more successful and sustainable generally. The various types of possible groups are: (i) Savings and Credit Groups, (ii) Social Forestry

Groups, (iii) Water Users' Groups, (iv) Watershed Development Groups, (v) Farmers' Interest Groups, etc.

SHG formation process

Before considering the formation of new groups, it is essential to understand the nature of existing groups in the society and the role of the poor in them. In many parts of India, it is possible to identify societies, where there are kinship groups or economic groups or activity groups already in existence, which may or may not undertake any organised development activity. Some examples of such groups are Grain, Fodder and Seed Banks in parts of Maharashtra, Madhya Pradesh and Orissa. The village kitties, joint forest management groups and village development committees in Uttar Pradesh.

Such existing groups can be identified and depending on their potential and suitability, elements of SHG approach can be introduced into these groups. Since these groups have some experience of collective working, it is easier to inculcate the saving habit in these groups. The formation of homogeneous groups of 10 to 20 persons may be promoted consisting of members who,

1. live under similar economic and social condition;
2. accept mutual responsibility for joint self help;
3. trust each other to such an extent that none of them would dominate or exploit the group.

Other factors which promote cohesiveness could be gender, occupational affinity, caste, etc. There is one member from one family in a group. In the new development initiative of group approach, it will be unrealistic to attempt group formation process without identifying and discussing the possible areas of common interests. At the same time offering packages or preplanned activities is contrary to the concept and practice of participatory development. The organisation of better opportunities for child and adult education, primary health care, literacy classes, etc. could serve as a 'entry point' for group formation. These activities require the organisation of people into associations and groups. During the awareness stage, various instruments like informal education, informal discussions, plays, puppet shows, etc. are used by NGOs to win over the confidence of the poor. The preparatory stage of awareness creation through various methods is very "time intensive" and in some cases may take up to a year.

Types of groups

Self-Help Groups (SHGs)

The group in this case does financial intermediation on behalf of the formal institution. This is the predominant model followed in India.

Grameen groups

In this model, financial assistance is provided to the individual in a group by the formal institution on the strength of group's assurance. In other words, individual loans are provided on the strength of joint liability/co-obligation. This microfinance model was initiated by Bangladesh Grameen Bank and is being used by some of the Microfinance Institutions (MFIs) in our country.

Problems in group formation

The process of group formation is time taking and complex involving social engineering. Many problems are faced during the process of formation and some of these are highlighted below:

- The group formation in many instances is opposed by well off people especially the moneylenders and socially dominant classes of rural population. The rural poor becoming a collective force is viewed as a threat to the existing socio-economic power relations in the village.
- There is resistance from men wherever the women groups are to be formed.

- Lack of common place and finding out a convenient time for holding meetings.
- Mental attitude of the rural poor tuned too much towards government programmes, subsidies and grants by NGOs or development agencies.

To overcome some of the problems, some of the NGOs follow a 'No Confrontation' approach and start working with the whole village. Then they slowly wean away the poor to subdivide into smaller primary activity groups. It is done in such a way that the richer peasantry either becomes indifferent to the groups or retains only the advisory role. Many NGOs find it easy to form women groups through entry points such as childcare and health programmes and then gradually initiate them into other activities. Moreover, in case of women groups, though there is opposition from men folk, the opposition from other sections of society is relatively less. In the formation or evolution of new SHGs, basically four stages are involved viz. pre-group formation, formation, performance and self-sustaining stage. It usually takes two to three years for SHGs to mature and reach the stage of self-sufficiency.

Self-Help Group sustainability

The group formation and functioning are not ends but means for development. If SHGs are to play their intended role, it is important that these emerge as sustainable entities. The group sustainability largely depends on the preparedness of group promoter and SHG members. If SHG members have been actively performing in a democratic and participatory mode with the spirit of self-help and financial discipline and SHG promoter has been successful in implementing its withdrawal strategy, sustainable SHGs will emerge. Such SHGs will continue to function without external support from the promoter.

Linking of SHGs with the vast network of formal Rural Financial Institutions (RFIs) including Commercial Banks,

Regional Rural Banks and Cooperative Banks is a potent way for evolution of sustainable SHGs. This is because both institutions, i.e. RFIs and SHGs are going to stay in the area whereas the NGOs who promote SHGs are going to withdraw in due course of time. In fact, the SHG-bank linkage begins with opening of saving bank account of the SHG in the nearby bank branch. However, credit linkage takes place after about six months mentioned earlier after proper appraisal or grading of the SHG by bank branch. Usually a cash credit limit is given for three years to the SHG depending on the level of group savings. The documentation is as prescribed by RBI. The drawing limit is usually up to four times of SHG saving as on date and is revised on annual basis.

The management of Self-Help Groups in a sustainable manner is a challenging task. It is interesting to note that SHGs with exclusive women members are more sustainable than those of men members. In fact, about 90 per cent SHGs that are linked to banks in India are of women members (NABARD website). This fact also augers well with the gender development issues in the country. However, the ultimate test of sustainability of SHG-bank linkage is that bankers start viewing SHGs as valuable customers for business purposes.

Current scene of SHG through bank linkage

Microfinance through SHGs has reached a commendable position and it is currently acknowledged as the biggest microfinance intervention in the world. The progress of the SHG-bank linkage programme since inception is shown below. Table 14.1 shows the number of SHGs linked to banks in India.

The programme took off with a humble beginning of linking 255 groups in the first year, i.e. 1992-93 with a loan disbursement of Rs. 2.9 million only. Average loan per SHG was about Rs. 11.37 thousand in 1992-93 whereas it has

Table 14.1 : No. of SHGs linked to banks in India

Year	Cumulative No. of SHGs	Bank Loan (Rs. Million)
1992-93	255	2.9
1993-94	620	6.5
1994-95	2,122	24.5
1995-96	4,757	60.6
1996-97	8,598	118.4
1997-98	14,317	237.6
1998-99	32,995	570.7
1999-2000	1,14,775	1929.8
2000-01	2,63,825	4809.0
2001-02	4,61,478	10263.0
2002-03	7,17,360	20487.0
2003-04	10,79,091	39042.0
2004-05	16,28,476	68984.6
2005-06	22,38,565	113980.0
2006-07	29,24,973	180410.0

Source: Various Reports of MCID, NABARD and NABARD website.

grown to Rs. 61.68 thousand in the year 2006-07. There has been a tremendous growth in the number of groups over time. More than 29.2 million SHGs with a membership of 40.95 million households are linked to bank credit till March 2007 as shown below. The Table 14.1 shows that there has been a rapid growth of SHGs that are linked with banks, i.e. Commercial Banks, Regional Rural Banks and Cooperative banks for meeting credit requirements and other financial needs of SHG members in recent years. Particularly after 2000 the number of SHGs linked to banks has grown exponentially. In addition, there is other experience, e.g. the Grameen Bank of Bangladesh model is being replicated in various parts of India. SIDBI is also promoting microfinance through NGOs, who are in the business of microfinance. Rashtriya Mahila Kosh (RMK) is also in the business of promoting microfinance in India through NGOs. It is estimated that the total outreach of Microfinance Institutions is about 7.5 million (Sa-Dhan website). If 40 million of SHG-bank linkage is added to this, the total outreach of microfinance in India would become truly significant keeping in mind that there are about 60 million poor households in India.

Impact of SHG-Bank Linkage Programme

Microfinancing, i.e. provisioning of small financial services and products to poor people is contributing to the process of development by creating conditions that are conducive to human development. It has a strong gender orientation. About 90 per cent SHGs that are linked to banks are reported to be of women as mentioned earlier. Through these groups, women empowerment is taking place. Their participation in economic activities and decision-making at household and at society level is increasing. It is making the process of development participatory, democratic, independent of subsidy and sustainable. Therefore, microfinance through SHGs is contributing to poverty reduction in a sustainable manner. It is reported that significant changes in the living standards of SHG members have taken place in terms of increase in income level, assets, savings, borrowing capacity and income generating activities. There are signs of empowerment taking place among women members of SHGs.

EMERGING CHALLENGES IN SHGs

The concept and results of microfinancing through SHGs thus are so impressive that it is attracting a lot of attention from all corners. There is a real danger that it may be hijacked by unwanted but otherwise influential agencies including government programmes. Also, a lot needs to be done for sustaining and upscaling the SHG movement. Some challenges that need to be addressed before microfinance through SHGs can significantly contribute to participatory rural development are outlined below:

- The number of SHGs linked to Banks has reached commendable height. However, many of these groups are not functioning properly. These groups need to be looked after. Normally, groups are promoted under certain programme or project. Once the programme or project is over, the agency withdraws and the groups are left on their own. Such groups need support for sustaining their efforts. This support is crucial and can prove to be vital for the long-term success of SHG-bank linkage programme.
- The participatory process of SHG formation is people-based and promotes self-help among the poor. The formation and maturity of SHGs depends on evolving group dynamics and can take up from one to three years. Therefore, hastening the process of SHG formation by setting unrealistic targets could do more harm than good.
- The true spirit of SHG evolution is in a direction away from subsidies. However, Swarnjayanti Gram Swarozgar Yojna (SGSY), a programme launched by Central Government since April 1999 is a credit-cum-subsidy program. Therefore, there is a danger of involving a subsidy-oriented programme in a movement which is, by and large, without any subsidy. There is a need to develop and implement guidelines for establishing linkages of SHGs with development programme such as SGSY so that subsidy is utilized properly without diluting the group cohesion.
- The process of rural development through SHGs is participatory and decentralized leading to empowerment of people. The vision is to have SHGs forming clusters and federation (association of clusters) for sustaining and up-scaling their operation. The need for clusters and federation arises due to the felt-need

of member-owned and member-managed institutions for sustainable rural development. Clusters and federations are being formed in many SHG-bank linkage related programmes. However, the process of cluster and federation promotion needs to be carefully designed and implemented with clear roles and responsibilities, be financial or non-financial, for sustainability of these institutions and also the future growth and sustainability of SHG-bank linkage programme.

- The process of group promotion is an important step in the process of sustainable SHG-bank linkage. Thus, the cost of group promotion has been paid by development agencies such as NABARD, other funding agencies, government agencies, etc. In future, more sustainable ways will have to be found for paying the cost of group promotion. One alternative is that banks pay the cost of group promotion either by training their own staff or hiring NGOs for doing the job of group formation for them. It is also possible that the villagers pay part of the cost. The point is that the cost has to be paid through sustainable means.
- Graduation of SHG members from taking consumption and production loans to availing loans for micro-enterprise development has to take place. This is essential for employment generation in rural areas. The SHG-bank linkage movement has to grow from self-employment to employment of some more people in the micro-enterprises run by SHG members. Capacity-building of SHG members and creation of backward and forward linkages for micro-enterprise development are crucial in this regard. The subsidy amount available under SGSY and other programs such as Agricultural Marketing Infrastructure (AMI) and National Rural Employment Guarantee Scheme

(NREGS) may be used for creating backward and forward linkages in rural areas.

- Lack of knowledge of the market and potential profitability, thus making the choice of business difficult.
- Inadequate book-keeping.
- Employment of too many relatives which increases social pressure to share benefits.
- Setting prices arbitrarily.
- Lack of capital.
- High interest rates.
- Inventory and inflation accounting is never undertaken.
- Credit policies that can gradually ruin their business.

All above challenges are real with which SHGs and change agents will have to struggle and find solutions for making SHGs suitable vehicles for sustainable microfinance services and eventually for sustainable rural development.

Conclusion

Majority of the women beneficiaries are not completely aware of the procedure of SHG scheme. The DRDA and banks have to conduct awareness programmes to improve awareness among rural women. SHG members have often lacked business skills and administrative capacity due to the inadequate provision of education and training. It is, therefore, essential on the part of the members. Hence, the government organs like DRDA and banks have to provide training facilities. In this regard, the non-government organizations and other associations should take initiative to make the women aware and motivate them towards self-employment. Further, women should be encouraged to start ventures confidently with enthusiasm by employing modern technology. They have to shift their line of activities on scientific and modern lines. The government should ensure a speedy change from traditional occupation to modern business enterprises in order to take the maximum benefit of new market conditions and technology. These measures, no doubt would certainly change traditional women and mould them as omnipotent.

REFERENCES

1. *Economic and Political Weekly* (2006), Increasing Concentration of Banking Operations, Vol. 41, No. 11, March, pp. 1113-1139.
2. *Economic Times*, New Delhi Edition, 29 August, 2005.
3. Mahajan, V. et al., (1999) "Dhakka starting microfinance in India" Chapter 29 in *Microfinance Emerging Challenges* (eds) K. Basu and K. Jindal, Tata McGraw, New Delhi.
4. Microcredit Innovations Department (MCID), NABARD, Mumbai, various reports.
5. MYRADA (2002), Impact of Self Help Groups (Group Processes) on the Social/Empowerment Status of Women in Southern India, NABARD, Mumbai, November.

15

A Macro Perspective on Microfinance

*Dr. G. Haranath
**Dr. Y. Subbarayudu

Introduction

Microfinance, also known as micro-credit, refers to the service of providing small amounts of money by financial institutions to the poor. These financial services may include savings, credit, insurance, leasing, money transfer, equity transaction, etc. provided to customers to help them meet their normal financial needs; with the only qualification that the transaction value is small and customers are poor.

The microfinance activity is the result of NABARD's work that started in 1992 through a pilot I project for promoting 500 self-help groups (SHGs). As the idea gained acceptance from the banking system and the results were promising, the Reserve Bank of India (RBI) encouraged this positive initiative by issuing instructions to banks in 1996 to cover SHG financing as a mainstream activity under their priority sector-lending portfolio.

* M.Com., M.B.A., M.F.T., M.F.M., Ph.D., Assistant Professor, Department of Commerce, Yogi Vemana University, Kadapa, Andhra Pradesh
** M.Com., M.B.A., Ph.D., Assistant Professor, Department of M.B.A., Yogi Vemana University, Kadapa-516003, Andhra Pradesh

The government of India made linking SHGs with banks a national priority from 1999 onwards through its periodic policy and budget announcements. NABARD continues to mature the outreach of the programme by providing umbrella support to stakeholders.

Today, the programme is growing at a pace of about 2.5 million households annually, It is the largest and the fastest growing microfinance programme in the world in terms of its outreach and sustainability. Internationally, the microfinance industry has had remarkable success in extending financial services to the poor.

Objectives of microfinance

Microfinance—as a miniscule but potentially significant and effective credit delivery system seeks to achieve the following broad range and multi-faceted objective to meet the credit needs of rural poor, including the non-bankable and landless.

- Support financial services to the rural poor, particularly enterprises who have not been able to secure the needed services from the formal financial system.
- Provide lendable and capacity building funds in respect of enterprises and various types of other grassroot level microfinance institutions.
- Support all initiatives for upscaling of the SHG-bank linking programmes through thrift-related banking activity.
- Build-up expertise in microfinance activities.
- To help build-up mutual trust and confidence between the bankers and the rural poor.
- To evolve supplementary strategy for meeting the credit needs of the poor by combining flexibility, sensitivity and responsiveness of the informal credit system with the strength of technical and administrative capabilities and financial resources of the formal credit institution.

Role of microfinance

The Indian microfinance is dominated by self-help groups and their linkage to banks with the launching of NABARD's pilot' scheme gained concepts like self-reliance, self-sufficiency and self-help at its core. Loans under microfinance programmes are very small in hundreds of rupees by Indian standards. Microfinance continues to target the rural and urban households, with emphasis on woman borrowers. Credit follows thrift the first stage is the formation of groups by individuals themselves, followed by the mobilization of petty savings and recycling this by lending to group members. The repayment period is generally very short. The amount increases based on the borrower's repayment. Group members usually create a common fund by contributing their small savings on regular basis. The average deposit and loan size of SHG account is larger than individual accounts under the priority sector. If banks provide proper training for skill and entrepreneurship development, the SHG members would be able to diversify into income generating activities, thus improving their credit adsorption capacity substantially.

Achievements of microfinance through SHGs

Microfinance programmes are important institutional devices for providing small credit to the rural poor in order to alleviate poverty. Microfinancing programmes through SHGs introduced and expanded by non-governmental organisations (NGOs) in several parts of India have the potential to minimize the problem of inadequate access of banking services to the poor. These can also influence savings.

Many of the studies reveal that increased availability of micro-credit to the poor through microfinancing SHGs will enable rural households to take up larger productive activities, empower the poor women, decrease the dependence on exploitative local moneylenders and increase savings.

Table 15.1: Progress according to model

Model Type	As on March 31, 2010	
	Number of SHGs (in '000)	Bank loans (in crores)
SHGs promoted, guided and financed by banks	343.37 (21%)	1,013 (15%)
SHGs promoted by NGOs/ government agencies and financed by banks	1,158.27 (72%)	5,529 (80%)
SHGs promoted by NGOs and financed by banks using NGOs/formal agencies as financial intermediaries	116.84 (7%)	356 (5%)
Total	**1,618.48**	**6,898**

Table 15.2: Progress through institutions

Agency	SHGs		Bank loan	
	Number	%	Amount	%
Commercial Banks	361,061	50	11,495	56
Regional Rural Banks	277,340	39	7,272	36
Cooperatives	78,959	11	1,720	8

Steps taken by the government

During the last year, the union government has taken the following steps for uplifting the microfinance sector.

1. The existing Micro-Finance Development Fund was redesigned as Micro-Finance Development and Equity Fund (MFDEF) and the corpus of the fund was increased from Rs. 100 crore to Rs. 200 crore. MFDEF is expected to play a vital role in capitalizing the microfinance institutions, thereby improving their access to commercial loans.
2. The central government is considering the need to identify and classify the microfinance institutions and rate such institutions to empower them to

intermediate between the lending banks and the clients.

3. The target for credit-linking to SHGs has been raised from 2 lakhs to 2.5 lakhs.
4. Draft bill on microfinance is proposed to be introduced in the next fiscal year.
5. An internal group of the Reserve Bank on rural credit and microfinance (under the chairmanship of H.R. Khan) was set up to examine the issues relating to microfinance.

Challenges in India

It has to be realized that microfinance is a means or an instrument for development, not an end itself. Assessing the extent to which India has been able to achieve the goal of poverty eradication and fulfill its role as a means for development requires indepth impact assessment on an ongoing basis.

Increasing amount of savings mobilization by microfinance institutions has to take place within a regulatory framework. In the absence of the same, unscrupulous elements may enter the sector and exploit the hard-earned savings of the poor.

Comparatively higher interest rate (12 to 36% per annum) charged by the microfinance institutions has again become a contentious issue. The high interest rate collected by the institutions from their poor clients is still perceived as exploitative in some quarters. The rate of interest has to be reduced.

The growth of microfinance institutions is constrained by the capacity of their staff and the availability of capital funds. Indian microfinance institutions depend on donor funds.

The industry has a long way to go as millions of low-income people remain unable to access formal financial services. In India, a very conservative estimate suggests that, at most, just 20 per cent of all the low-income people have access to financial services from formal financial institutions, microfinance institutions and other such stakeholders.

Suggestions for future development

NABARD as a strategic policy have pioneered in formulation of development programmes together with appropriate guidelines in the areas of microfinance. This has been possible through continuous innovation based on programme approach linking support organisations with the credit institutions essential support mechanism and Non-Governmental Organisation for strengthening microfinance activities in the country.

- To ensure and facilitate the increase of the reach of the existing and new microfinance groups institutions.
- To help strengthen the capacity of both promoting and implementing agencies.
- To establish linkages with implementing and supporting agencies.
- A non-governmental body with representation from banks, the Government, NGOs and microfinance institutions.

Conclusion

Microfinance helps the rural poor to improve their standard of living and fulfills their credit needs. Hence the self-help groups are a new innovation in the field of rural development to finance the rural poor and also to satisfy their credit needs. Rural economy helps in improving the economic status of the each and every individual in the rural area.

REFERENCES

1. Harper, Malcolm, 2002, "Promotion of Self Help Groups under the SHG Bank Linkage Program in India", Paper presented at the Seminar on SHG-Bank Linkage Programme at New Delhi, November 25-26, 2002.

2. Bansal, Hema, 2003, "SHG-Bank Linkage Program in Indian: An Overview", *Journal of Microfinance*, Vol. 5, Number 1.
3. Rajesh Chakrabarti, *The Indian Microfinance Experience – Accomplishments and Challenges*—An article.
4. Dr. R. Suneetha "Is DWACRA Programme Empowering the Rural Women?" *Kurukshetra*, Vol. 55.
5. http://www.empowering-women.com/schemedetails.asp?IngSchemeID=77
6. http://www.worldbank.org/participation/APDPIP_case.pdf)
7. http://www.indev.nic.in/need/activities.html

16

Empowerment and Entrepreneurship

A Glance at Successful Women Entrepreneurs through SHGs in Kadapa District

*Dr. P. Saritha
**Dr. G. Vijaya Bharathi
***Mr. P. Harinatha Reddy

ABSTRACT

In every society women play a crucial role. Whenever women have been given a charge, they have not only excelled in all areas but they have also played an important role in the development of the society. To accelerate the overall growth and prosperity of the nation, it is very important to create opportunities for socio-economic development of women. It is high time that the developing nations utilize their women force to the optimum level. It is imperative to note that men alone cannot break the shackles of poverty, unemployment, inequality and population explosion. Active and equal participation of women in the accomplishment of this herculean task is indispensable. With the qualities of dedication, hard work, perseverance and honesty women are capable of

* Assistant Professor, Department of MBA, YV University, Kadapa-516 003
** Assistant Professor, Department of Commerce, YV University, Kadapa-516 003
*** Research Scholar, Department of Commerce, Sri Venkateswara University, Tirupati-517 502, (A.P.)

producing much better results than men. Economic independence of women will create far reaching social changes and prove a necessary weapon for them to face injustice and discrimination. At this critical juncture, self-employment is the only solution to generate income for them. The whole purpose of economic advancement is to improve the quality of life of people and the quality of life of women. Therefore, the income generated through self-employment might help the individual to improve the quality of life.

Hence, the paper concentrates on various case studies of women entrepreneurs through SHGs in Kadapa district, A.P. in India. The Self-Help Group [SHG] is considered as a voluntary association of poor people. The implicit objective of SHGs is to combat unjust social relationship by increasing people's participation through their empowerment. The emphasis is also on human resource and entrepreneurship development. Shakeela Self-Help Group case study presents ***Best Practices Make Perfect****, Sri Lakshmi Swayam Sahayaka Sangham case study gives a light on* ***Cheekatilo Chiru Divvelu*** *(Lights in the Dark), Anajaneyapuram case study is a model for* ***Enterprises for Empowerment,*** *Avalasettigaripalli case study is a great paradigm for* ***Success through New Designs****. Even though there are number of successful entrepreneurs in the Kadapa district, the paper concentrated only on few case studies and provides some recommendations for women entrepreneurship development and empowerment in the Kadapa district in particular and in India in general.*

Introduction

An entrepreneur is a key figure in economic progress. He/she is the person who introduces new things in the economy. The entrepreneur is considered as the business leader and not as simple owner of the capital. The entrepreneur is a person with telescopic faculty, drive and talent who perceives business opportunities and promptly seizes them for exploitation. Entrepreneurship is the ability to create and build something from practically nothing. Fundamentally, a human creative activity, finding personal energy by initiating, building and achieving an enterprise or organization rather than by just watching, analyzing or describing one. It requires the ability to take calculated risk and reduce the chance of failure. It is the ability to build a founding team to complement the entrepreneurial skill and talents. In our country, entrepreneurship movement is gathering momentum now-a-days and a plethora of support agencies are coming forward to drive the movement a long way for success. A high sense of responsibility is an essential ingredient for development of entrepreneurship in India. As such:

Entrepreneurship = Entrepreneur + Enterprise
↓ ↓ ↓
process person object

Characteristics of entrepreneurship

Entrepreneurship as an economic activity emerges and functions in socio-economic and cultural settings. It is a complex and multifaceted subject. The following are the important characteristics of entrepreneurship:

Decision-making

Decision making activity is one of the fundamental characteristic features of entrepreneurship. A decision is a course of action which is consciously chosen from among a multiple of alternatives to achieve the desired result. As entrepreneurship involves both risk and uncertainty, decision-making is crucial on the part of the entrepreneurs to establish and run the enterprise successfully.

Accepting challenges

Entrepreneurship means accepting challenges, risk and uncertainty. While accepting entrepreneurship as a career, the entrepreneur accepts the challenges of all odds and puts his efforts to convert the odds into viable business opportunities by pooling together the resources for building and running the enterprise.

Risk taking

One of the important characteristics of entrepreneurship is risk taking or risk bearing. This characteristic feature implies assuming the responsibility for loss that may occur due to unforeseen contingencies of the future. Entrepreneur, by his deep insight and scientific approach, analyses the situation objectively and reduces the risk considerably on one hand and enhances the profit factor on the other.

Building organisation

Entrepreneurship presupposes the initiative and skill on building organization. It is by delegation of authorities and proper leadership that organization can be built up. Organization-building is the most critical skill needed for entrepreneurship as it facilitates the economic use of other innovations.

Skilful management

Entrepreneurship involves skillful management. The basic managerial skill is the most important characteristic feature of entrepreneurship. For effective management of an enterprise, the role of an entrepreneur to initiate and supervise design of organization-improvement projects in relation to upcoming opportunities is very much important.

Innovation

The two important characteristics of entrepreneurship are, first doing things in a new and better way and secondly, decision-making under uncertainty. So, innovation is one of the most important characteristics of entrepreneurship.

Mobilization of resources

Resources mobilization is also a fundamental characteristic feature of entrepreneurship. Resources are the help needed to carry out activities resulting in accomplishment of goal. They are found in scattered manner in the environment and required to be perceived, identified and mobilized by entrepreneurs to attain business goal. Thus, entrepreneurs make themselves distinct from the rest of population because of their innate capability to mobilize resources. This is because resources are needed to ensure success which has the highest priority in the minds of entrepreneurs.

Concept of SHGs

Women empowerment and entrepreneurship through SHG based microfinance has been a central point to development agenda in India. Indian government has also paid special attention to women's empowerment and entrepreneurship. Women's empowerment encompasses their enhanced status in social, political and economic spheres. The Self-Help Group [SHG] is considered as a voluntary association of poor people. They are mostly having some socio-economic background. They are involved in solving their common problems through self-help and mutual help. It creates small saving among the members and the amounts are kept with any bank. The SHGs have a membership of 15 to 20 members. A self-help group is also defined as a voluntary group valuing personal interaction and mutual aid as means of altering or ameliorating problems perceived as alterable pressing and personal by most of its members.

The concept of SHG is to encourage collective learning, promote leadership, address common constraints to create awareness among the growers; trainee with the financial institutions/NGOs/Government agencies to mobilise required technical and financial resources and encourage on-farm and non-farm micro-enterprise activities among the members of the group. The implicit objective of SHGs is to combat unjust social relationship by increasing people's participation through their empowerment. The emphasis is also on human resource and entrepreneurship development. The SHGs are generally of small size. Such small sized SHGs not only ensure active participation, but also promote group dynamics in decision-making and greater transparency. Moreover, separate SHGs for men and women are more conducive for addressing the issues of gender imbalances. Also SHGs frame their own rules and regulations to suit their local conditions. Though the primary objective of microfinance interventions is to help the poor to surmount poverty, they also assist them to undertake financially viable enterprises, which could be taken up by the banks for commercial lending.

SUCCESSFUL SHG WOMEN ENTREPRENEURS IN KADAPA DISTRICT

A case study on "Best Practices Make Perfect"

The growth and development of any sector depends upon the best practices those are adopted and practiced in that particular sector and the same would apply for the SHG movement, which aimed at poverty alleviation and community empowerment through establishment of poor peoples' institutions. The clarity in goals and objectives of Self-Help groups will determine the pace and direction of their development. Hence the groups among rural poor must be facilitated based on long-term goals rather than for short-term pecuniary gains. The DRDA-Kadapa has carefully facilitated the best practices among the SHGs for long-term sustainability of the groups to achieve the anticipated benefits. Shakeela SHG of Y. Kota village is one of the examples for the best practices of a good SHG.

Y. Kota village is one of the most backward and remote villages in Kadapa district. The DRDA-Kadapa has formed about 10 SHGs in village with the objectives of poverty alleviation through women empowerment and entrepreneurship. Shakeela Self-Help Group is one of the such 10 groups, which has been formed during 1999 in the Y. Kota village. Other groups in the village and in the groups across the mandal see this group as role model and try to learn from the practices the group is following. The Shakeela group is an example to motivate the other groups in the mandal as well as in the district.

Shakeela group comprises 10 members who hail from same community, occupation and have similar economical, social problems. The group members themselves decided, who should be their group members and not the DRDA staff. The self-selection of members helped them for having strong cohesiveness and unity and helped the group in avoiding the entrance of vested interest people and potential defaulters.

The group meets every 3rd of the month at a pre-decided place in which they deposit savings, take loans, repay the loan amounts and interest, take decisions to facilitate the smooth functioning of the group. As a result all the group members know who is taking loan and who is repaying. The group leader Ms. Sheik Badarunnissa said that neither she responsible for sanctioning the loan nor enforcement of the repayment. She says, "Group collectively take a decision who should be given and how much should be given and not the leaders. This practice helped me not to become accountable for collection of repayments like in some of the groups where leader is responsible for advancing loans and at the same time collection of repayments.

The group members proudly said that they know how to manage their corpus fund effectively and efficiently. They have started loaning activity from the very beginning of the group formation. They advance loans based upon the needs of the members after thorough discussion on the need, purpose, the repayment procedure, interest and the like. The repayment rate in the group is always more than 98 per cent because of the groups' rigorous approach in loan processing, utilization monitoring and enforcement practices. The group members said that they won't accept one-time repayments, hence each member has to repay the loans in monthly installments as per their income levels and the members can repay more money if they have excess income.

The group has comprehensive and simple record-keeping system by which each member knows total savings, loan outstanding, installment amount, interest etc. The group members were trained on book-keeping system and at the end of each meeting the group leaders announce how much saving, principle amount and interest collected, who were given loans, the important decisions taken by the group etc. in that particular meeting. Initially the group members felt all this as an uninteresting and a waste of time but subsequently they strongly felt that it is an essential activity in each meeting to ensure transparency in the group. The local branch of Syndicate Bank has sanctioned direct loan to this group by seeing the best practices followed by this group. Ms. Shaik Tehera, the secretary of the group has said that all the members of their group have immense trust in the group and self-discipline because of the practices they have adopted and now these practices have been institutionalized.

A case study on *Cheekatilo Chiru Divvelu* (Lights in the Dark)

The greatest contribution of Self-Help Group in the face of their fight against deprivation and poverty is that it empowers them by their increased critical self-awareness giving them a feeling of self-confidence, solidarity and social security to control and guide their own destinies. Kadapa is one of the backward districts in the state of Andhra Pradesh where the rainfall is about 640 ml, much less than the average rainfall in the state. Majority of the population depend upon rainfed agriculture.

The DRDA-Kadapa has formed over 13,000 SHGs in the district with the consistent efforts by District Rural Development Agency. "Sri Lakshmi Swayam Sahayaka Sangham" is one of the SHGs formed during 1999. About 15 women from below the poverty line families of Akkayaapalli came together and formed a SHG. "In the initial days we have never believed that we could save continuously and take loans from the group and earn enough money to run our families, we have just formed the group with the hope of getting DRDA grant but because of the payback we have tasted by participating in SHG now we want to continue in the group for ever" says Mrs. Dastagirimma with great confidence and overflowing satisfaction.

Initially the group used to save Rs.30 per month and they have opened SB Account in Rayalaseema Grameena Bank and started advancing their savings as loans among the group members. The DRDA-Kadapa has provided Rs. 10,000 as revolving fund by which the group could advance larger volumes of loans to the members. The group members have started small enterprises individually by using the advances. During this time the DRDA has organized an exposure visit for the group to the Kurnool district, where group members collectively making soft toys and earning profit. After that the group members have decided to do a collective activity instead of small individual businesses. The Group has identified food processing is a potential enterprise and with the DRDA support they got trained on food processing like making Masala Powder, Chilli Powder, Ragi Powder and the like.

Fig. 16.1: Members of Sri Lakshmi Swayam Sahayaka Sangham on Collective Work

As the food-processing unit requires more financial assistance the group has approached the bank for financial assistance under NABARD propagated SHG-Bank Linkage

Program and got Rs. 25,000 financial assistance. The group has started making powders and sell the products in the local shops, shandies etc. Meanwhile the state government has started the "Rythu Bazars" in all the towns and Mandal Headquarters where farmers can directly sell their products without any mediators help. The group has approached the district administration and got the permission to establish their outlet in the Rythu Bazar, which helped them in saving lot of money otherwise they need to give to local general stores.

Most recently the state government has announced the new scheme called "Gruha Mitra" (Fair Price Shop) where the families can buy the food products at reasonable rates. The group has again approached the Joint Collector of the district and got permission to supply food material to four such "Gruha Mitra" shops. Each member is earning about Rs. 2500 per month and the group corpus fund has been steadily increasing day by day to meet the growing credit needs of the members. The group has availed Rs. 50,000 loan from the bank under SHG-Bank Linkage refinance program.

When asked about their future plan the group members confidently said that they are not all worried about the basic family needs and moreover they can take care of their children education, health etc on their own and they said, *"Maakippudu Chala Dhiryam vochindi repu emi avuntandane bhayam maku ledu ma jeevitalu ela bagu chesukovalo maku telsu"* (Now we have great confidence on us and we are no more worried about tomorrow and we know how to develop our lives).

A case study on "Enterprises for Empowerment"

"Just eight years ago it was a tiny village with thatched houses with all daily laborers and now the scenario has changed significantly. The village has become as role model for surrounding villages with the ecstatic women entrepreneurs". This success story is one of the illustrations created by the women SHGs promoted under DWCRA scheme implemented by the DRDA-Kadapa of Andhra Pradesh. Anjaneyapuram is one of the small villages situated in Chakrayapet mandal in Kadapa district of Andhra Pradesh. The village comprised about 50 families of which majority of them belong to weavers community and remaining families belong to other backward classes. The weavers' families used to work as daily labors at the master weavers who actually located in nearby town. During 1994 the DRDA has entered the village with the concept of Self-Help Groups under the DWCRA schemes. With the constant persuasion from the DRDA staff some of the women formed as an SHG with the name of "Sri Rajeswari SHG" and started saving monthly from the little they could earn out of labor. The remaining women in the village also formed in to SHGs with in short-span of time by seeing the first group.

Now there are around 40 women, participating in SHG movement in three SHGs. The members were trained on how to transform the little savings in to loans and women started using them for purchasing the raw material for weaving the cloth and slowly started reducing the number of working days devoted for the master weavers of the nearby town but this could not solve their problem because their savings were very little compare to their investment needs. In this juncture the DRDA-Kadapa has provided Rs. 15,000 as revolving loan fund to each group to boost up their self-confidence from which the members could obtain bigger loans and utilized as working capital. As a result the weavers families completely stopped working for the master weavers as daily laborers and started producing material on their own.

The DRDA staff has educated the women about the other opportunities available to increase their working capital and as a result the SHGs have availed the bank loans at lower interest rates under SHG-Bank linkage program. Some of the Group members were taken up Bangle selling business by taking NABARD finance. With the increased income the families could build pucca houses, which is further, increased their productivity in better and safe environment. The women started collective procurement of the raw material and marketing the produce without depending upon the master weavers. Ms. Sunanda, the leader of the Chowdeswari says "the SHG has saved us from the scrupulous moneylenders and the exploitative master weavers, who have eaten away all our surplus money for so many years, thanks to DWCRA scheme which helped us to live with self-respect and unity.

A case study on "Success through New Designs"

Avalasettigaripalli is a small remote backward village in Galiveedu mandal, 75 km away from Kadapa. The village consist of 200 BC families of Balija caste and nearly 100 families of SCs. Most of the families are below the poverty line. The main occupation of the village is Thunga Mat Weaving. The women of the village used to work under master weavers for labour of Rs. 2 to 3 per mat. Some of the families were doing mat weaving individually by taking loan from the moneylenders. During the year 1999 the DRDA has formed seven SHGs with the women of the village with a minimum savings of Rs. 30 per month. All the seven SHGs have been provided RF of Rs. 15,000 from DRDA side and 1st dose NABARD finance from local RG Bank. The women started weaving individually by taking loans from their group. They used to purchase raw material locally and marketed the products to Salem (Tamilnadu).

During the month of August 2002 the DRDA has imported training on New Designs and value addition by designer from Alkamist Visual Studio Pvt. Ltd., Hyderabad. Now the Mats prepared with Thunga in different shapes and designs are being exhibited at Hyderabad in Gift Exhibition and as well as Family World Exhibition. As a result bulk orders have come from Malasia and as well as Hospitals and Yoga institutes of Hyderabad.

The above customers ready to pay Rs. 75-200 based upon the size and design of the mat. The DRDA has sanctioned a Jakard mission and one community hall for creating the good working environment. Because of the training in new designs, the mat weavers are getting 100 per cent more price for the same cost of the raw material and labour. The success of this value addition program has enhanced the income levels.

Recommendations for women entrepreneurs development

The following recommendations are suggested for the women entrepreneurs to work with patience, perseverance, self-confidence and courage and to overcome all the hurdles and also to come up in their life:

- Women should come forward to do self-employment irrespective of their marital status and education.
- Women should avoid being idle and be ready to learn new crafts like tailoring, beautician courses, hand works etc.
- Women can work as groups and help each other.
- Women entrepreneurs should make use of the incentives schemes offered by the government.
- Women entrepreneurs should have complete knowledge of their product and their ability.
- Government should improve publicity regarding the incentive/concessions and organize more awareness programmes to women entrepreneurs through various media.
- Government should encourage private training institutions involved in women entrepreneurs.
- Government should reduce the procedural difficulties.
- Women associations should come forward to participate in women entrepreneurs development.
- Women entrepreneurs should be encouraged and must have enough knowledge to avail the concessions offered by the nationalized banks, state financing corporations and other state agencies.
- Government banks and financial institutions should come forward to offer loan to women entrepreneurs with attractive low interest rates and simplified procedures.
- Market support and preferential treatment may be given to women entrepreneurs in the society.

REFERENCES

1. Kulshrestha, L.R. and Gupta, A., *SHG Bank Linkage: A New Paradigm for Combating Poverty in Globalization Growth and Poverty*, Serials Publications, New Delhi, 2004.

2. DRDA Annual Reports, Kadapa district, 2009 & 10.
3. www.statebankofindia.org
4. *Journal Rural Development*
5. *Journal of Management Researcher*
6. *EENAADU* Newspaper, December, 2009.

17

Women Entrepreneurship
An Outlook

*Mr. P. Harinatha Reddy
**Mrs. Reddy Lakshmi
***Dr. S.V. Subba Reddy

ABSTRACT

Entrepreneurship development is the key factor to fight against unemployment, poverty and to prepare ourselves for globalization in order to achieve overall Indian economic progress. The scope of entrepreneurship development in country like India is tremendous. In India, where over 900 million people are living, 300 million are below the poverty line. It is simply impossible for any government to provide means of livelihood to every one. In such a situation entrepreneurship is the only source through which the problem of unemployment can be eradicated. Women in business are a recent phenomenon in India. Entrepreneurship is a more suitable profession for women than regular employment in public and private sectors since they have to fulfill dual roles. Women have been taking increasing interest in recent years in income

* Research Scholar, Department of Commerce, Sri Venkateswara University, Tirupati-517 502, A.P.

** Research Scholar, Department of Commerce, Sri Venkateswara University, Tirupati-517 502, A.P.

*** Department of MBA (HRM), Yogi Vemana University, Kadapa-516 003

generating activities, self-employment and entrepreneurship. The status of women in India has been changing as a result to growing industrialisation and urbanisation, spasmodic mobility and social legislation. The government of India has also stressed on special entrepreneurship programmes and several schemes for women with a view to encourage more and more women enterprises and to uplift their economic status. Some efforts have been taken into account for the effective development of women entrepreneurs such as better educational facilities, adequate training programme on management skills, encourage women's participation in decision-making, vocational training, women's polytechnics and industrial training institutes, training on professional competence and leadership skill. Women entrepreneurship must be moulded properly with entrepreneurial traits and skills to meet the changes in trends, challenges, global markets and also be competent enough to sustain and strive for excellence in the entrepreneurial arena.

Introduction

In this dynamic world, women entrepreneurs are an important part of the global quest for sustained economic development and social progress. In India, though women have played a key role in the society, their entrepreneurial ability has not been properly tapped due to the lower status of women in the society. It is only from the Fifth Five Year Plan (1974-78) onwards that their role has been explicitly recognized with a marked shift in the approach from women welfare to women development and empowerment. The development of women entrepreneurship has become an important aspect of our plan priorities. Several policies and programmes are being implemented for the development of women entrepreneurship in India. Over the years, the phenomenon of women entrepreneurship is largely confined only to metropolitan cities at big towns in India. In order to achieve the objective of social justice. it is necessary to harness the latent skills and potentials of women. It is recognized that women have to play a key role in the overall economic development of the country. Though, women represent almost half of our country's total population but the literacy rate of women remains at the level of 39.29 per cent against 64.13 per cent of their counterparts as per 2001 census at the country level. Our late Prime Minister, Smt. Indira Gandhi said, "No society could progress unless women, who contribute half of its population, were given equal opportunities". Even after decades of independence the position of women entrepreneurs has not improved in our country, in spite of the pledge made in the Constitution of India for equality of opportunities.

In recent times, women of India have taken commendable part in the field of entrepreneurship. Entrepreneurship is a more suitable profession for women than regular employment in public and private sectors since they have to fulfill dual roles. They are exploration of the prospects of starting a new business enterprise, undertaking of risks and the handling of economic uncertainties involved in business, introduction or imitation of innovations, coordination, administration, control and supervision and also leadership. At present, their estimated number is 12.99 lakh women managed enterprises. Women are taking up both traditional activities and also non-traditional activities. First National Conference of Women Entrepreneurs held at New Delhi in November 1981 advocated the need for developing women entrepreneurs for the overall development of the country. It called for priority to women in allotment of land, sheds, sanction of power, licensing and the like. The second International Conference of Women Entrepreneurs organized by the National Alliance of Young Entrepreneurs (NAYE) held in 1989 at New Delhi also adopted certain declarations involving women's participation in industry.

Opportunities for women entrepreneur

Our late Prime Minister, Smt. Indira Gandhi said, "No society could progress unless women, who contribute half of its population, were given equal opportunities". Even after decades of independence the position of women entrepreneurs has not improved in our country, in spite of the pledge made in the Constitution of India for equality of opportunities. Women entry into business is a new phenomenon. Considering the flow of women entrepreneurs in the traditional and conventional industries and product lines, it is often criticized that the women entrepreneurship in India is caught up in "3Ps". Women entrepreneurship is traced out as an extension of their kitchen activities to three Ps, i.e., pickles, powder (masala) and pappad manufacturing. With growing awareness and spread of education over the years, women have started engrossing to modern activities, popularly known as three Es—engineering, electronics and energy.

In urban areas

Some important opportunities are identified for the women in urban areas are: computer services and information dissemination, trading in computer stationery, computer maintenance, travel and tourism, quality testing, poster and indoor plant library, recreation centers for old people, culture centers, screen printing, photography and video shooting, stuffed soft toys, wooden toys, mini laundry, community eating centers, community kitchens, job contract for packaging of goods, beauty parlours, communications centers like STD booths, cyber cafes, catering services and health clubs and the like.

In semi-urban areas

Considering the socio-economic, cultural and educational status and the motivation of women in semi-urban, particularly projects with low investments, low technical know-how and assured market are suggested for the improvement of opportunities identified for semi-urban women are production of liquid soap, soap power, detergent, deodorants, office stationery like cushion pads, gum, and ink pads, convenience, readymade, instant food products including pickles, spices, pappads, community services, child-care centers and culture centers for children, nursery classes and manufacturing of leather goods and the like.

In rural areas

In the recent industrial policy, the government has given tremendous importance for the agro-based and allied products. Only one to two per cent of the total production of fruits and vegetables is processed every year in India. This reveals a huge scope for the food, fruit and vegetable processing industry. Women have a natural flair and instinct for food preparing and processing. A new market is developed for the processed fruits and vegetables in the form of baby foods, ice cream, convenience food, cold drinks, canned products traditional medicine preparation and the like. Thus, there are plenty of opportunities available for women entrepre-neurs.

Types of industries managed by women

In recent years, women entrepreneurs have entered all the fields of business and industry. In the last decade, there has been a remarkable shift from the manufacturing industry to the service industry. The figure 17.1 gives the overall account of products for women entrepreneurs. It is observed that educational background and experience has little or no effect on the choice of selection of business opportunity.

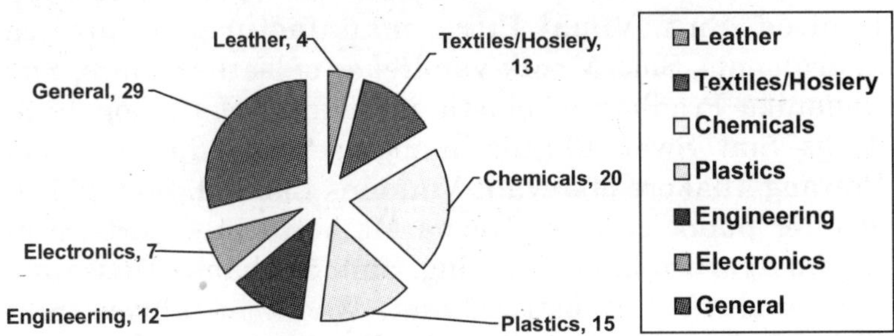

Fig. 17.1: Type of Industries Selected by Women Entrepreneurs

Table 17.1: Work participation of women in India

Year (Census)	Percentage
1971	14.2
1981	19.7
1991	22.3
2001	31.6

Source: http:// www.ebbf.org/woman.htm.

From Table 17.1 it is to be observed that the percentage of work participation of women in business shown in increasing trend from 14.2 per cent in 1971 to 31.6 in 2001 census. It seems the growth depends upon the programmes and schemes which are provided by the Government and also financial support given by the financial institutions.

Some examples of successful women entrepreneurs

Although the list of successful women entrepreneurs is quite long, selected representative women entrepreneurs are mentioned here. They have attributed their success in their enterprise to hard work, perseverance, dedication, devotion, determination, integrity and confidence in themselves. The successful and accomplished women entrepreneurs are Smt. Sumati Mararji of Shipping Corporation been seen as beacon to women entrepreneurs. Smt. Sharayu Daftary of automobile radiators, Smt.Yamutai Kirloskar of Mahila Udyog Limited, Smt. Vimal Pitre, manufacturer of surgical instruments, Smt. Manik Vandrekar of leather crafts, Smt. Radanika Pradhan of plastic industries, Smt. Gogate for drugs, Smt. Swati Bhatija in engineering industries, Smt. Prerang Thakore of Jayant Vitamins Limited, Smt. Nargis of inter publicity, Smt. Neena Malhotra in exports, Smt. Rajani Agarwal in engineering, Smt. Shahanaz Hussain in beauty clinical cosmetics, Smt. Wadia in fabrics, Smt. Weheeda Rehman in fast foods all stand out as successful women entrepreneurs. Other outstanding women entrepreneurs – Smt. Priya Khanna, Smt. Savitri Debi, Smt. Raman Suri, Smt. Madhra Chatrapathy, Smt. Prabha Thakkar, Smt. Sunanda Pant and the like.

Supportive measures for women entrepreneurship development

Right measures from all areas are required in the development of women entrepreneurs and their greater participation in the entrepreneurial activities. To attune the young minds to business enterprise, entrepreneurship education should be imparted in secondary schools and colleges as well as universities with special emphasis on women. Women should be made aware of various credit facilities, financial incentives and subsidies. Government should take initiative to organize large numbers of cooperative societies of women entrepreneurs and also support system should streamline and reorient their programmes and policies in a direction leading to higher job involvement, higher achievement motivation and lesser role conflict among women entrepreneurs. To make it possible active policy intervention for better infrastructure, adequate finance, better market facilities is a must. Successful women in the field of entrepreneurship have to help other women in starting and sustaining in their business whole-heartedly. The following are the supportive measures to develop women entrepreneurship and their economic status.

Direct and indirect financial support

Support system should streamline and reorient their programmes and policies in a direction leading to higher job involvement, higher achievement motivation and lesser role conflict among women entrepreneurs. To make it possible active policy intervention for better infrastructure, adequate finance, better market facilities is a must. Women should be made aware of various credit facilities, financial incentives and subsidies. District Industries Centres and Single Window Agencies should make use of assisting women in their trade and business guidance.

- Nationalized banks
- State finance corporation
- State industrial development corporation
- District industries centers
- Differential rate schemes
- Mahila Udyug Needhi scheme
- Small Industries Development Bank of India (SIDBI)
- State Small Industrial Development Corporations (SSIDCs)

Yojana schemes and programme

More governmental schemes to motivate women entrepreneurs to engage in small-scale and large-scale business ventures. Government should take initiative to organize large numbers of cooperative societies of women entrepreneurs. Special training-cum-orientation programmes are needed for those employees and officer who are supposed to help women entrepreneurs.

- Nehru Rojgar Yojana
- Jacamar Rojgar Yojana
- TRYSEM
- DWACRA

Technological training and awards

To support and supplement women entrepreneurship, it should be in the form of training—skill upgradation, managerial skills, production and marketing along with development programmes like health and nutrition, women and child welfare and the like.

- Stree Shakti Package by SBI
- Entrepreneurship Development Institute of India
- Trade Related Entrepreneurship Assistance and Development (TREAD)

- National Institute of Small Business Extension Training (NSIBET)
- Women's University of Mumbai

Federations and associations

The National Alliance of Young Entrepreneurs (NAYE) has a separate wing for women entrepreneurs. The World Association of Women Entrepreneurs (WAWE) was very anxious to set up joints ventures in India. Other world wide associations such the International Alliance and the International Business and Professional Women's Association are also well known. All of these organizations aim to bring together women in business to help them achieve their business goals. In addition to the above association, Self-Employed Women's Association (SEWA) of Ahmedabad are doing considerable work for the benefit of women entrepreneurs. SNDT Women's University of Bombay conducts post-graduate diploma course for women in banking, travel, tourism etc.

- National Alliance of Young Entrepreneurs (NAYE)
- India Council of Women Entrepreneurs, New Delhi
- Self Employed Women's Association (SEWA)
- World Association of Women Entrepreneurs (WAWE)
- Associated Country Women of the World (ACWW)

Conclusion

Today, it is universally recognized that women entrepreneurs have to bear the force of socio-economic advancement since advanced countries are still profiteering from the contributions of women entrepreneurship. The Non-Governmental Organizations have a bigger role in stimulating and nurturing the spirit of entrepreneurship amongst women. The new industrial policy of Government of India has specially highlighted the need for special entrepreneurship development for women entrepreneurs in the nature of product-process-oriented courses to enable them to start small-scale industries. If the development can be able to successfully utilize the women force then the total development will be easy and sex discrimination, economic oppression and social stratification can be removed. The government has taken measures for enlistment of women. Efforts are on at the government and voluntary agencies levels to tap the hitherto unrecognized and unaccounted strength of women to integrate them in the process of industrial development, more especially small-scale industry development in the country. Women entrepreneurship must be moulded properly with entrepreneurial traits and skills to sustain and strive for excellence in the entrepreneurial arena. Government has realized that the women entrepreneurship and EDPs are effective instruments for fostering industrial development and to boosts the process of structural diversification, modernization, self-reliance of the country economy.

REFERENCES

1. Ganesa Murthy, V.S. (2008), *Empowerment of Women in India*, New Century Publications, New Delhi.
2. http:// www.ebbf.org/woman.htm.
3. http://www.unido.org/doc
4. Narayana Barua and Aparajeetha Borkakoty (2005), *Women Entrepreneurship*, APH Publishing Corporation, New Delhi.

18

Women Empowerment through Microfinance

*Nagaraja, G.

ABSTRACT

In India, the emergence of liberalization and globalization in early 1990s aggravated the problem of women workers in unorganized sectors from bad to worse as most of the women who were engaged in various self-employment activities have lost their livelihood. Despite tremendous contribution of women in the agriculture sector, their work is considered just an extension of household domain and remains non-monetised.

Microfinance interventions are well-recognized world over as an effective tool for poverty alleviation and improving socio-economic status of rural poor. In India too, microfinance is making headway in its effort for reducing poverty and empowering rural women. Microfinance through the network of cooperatives, commercial banks, regional rural banks, NABARD and NGOs has been largely supply-driven and a recent approach. Microfinance institutions are, other than banks, are engaged in the provision of financial services to the poor. Microfinance is emerging as a powerful instrument for poverty alleviation in the new economy. In India, Microfinance scene is dominated by Self-Help Group (SHGs)-Bank Linkage Programme as a cost-effective mechanism for providing

* Assistant Professor, Department of Economics, SVUPG Centre, Kavali

financial services to the "Unreached Poor" which has been successful not only in meeting financial needs of the rural poor women but also strengthen collective self-help capacities of the poor, leading to their empowerment. Rapid progress in SHG formation has now turned into an empowerment movement among women across the country. Economic empowerment results in women's ability to influence or make decision, increased self-confidence, better status and role in household etc. Microfinance is necessary to overcome exploitation, create confidence for economic self-reliance of the rural poor, particularly among rural women who are mostly invisible in the social structure.

This paper puts forward how microfinance has received extensive recognition as a strategy for economic empowerment of women. This paper seeks to examine the impact of Microfinance with respect to poverty alleviation and socio-economic empowerment of rural women. An effort is also made to suggest the ways to increase women empowerment

Introduction

Empowerment implies expansion of assets and capabilities of people to influence control and hold accountable institution that affects their lives (World Bank Resource Book). Empowerment is the process of enabling or authorizing an individual to think, behaves, take action and control work in an autonomous way. It is the state of feelings of self-empowered to take control of one's own destiny. It includes both controls over resources (physical, human, intellectual and financial) and over ideology (belief, values and attitudes) (Batliwala, 1994).

Empowerment can be viewed as a means of creating a social environment in which one can take decisions and make choice either individually or collectively for social transformation. It strength innate ability by way of acquiring knowledge power and experience.

Empowerment is a multi-dimensional social process that helps people gain control over their own lives, communities and their society, by acting on issues that they define as important. Empowerment occurs within sociological, psychological economic spheres and at various levels, such as individual, group and community and challenges our assumptions about status quo, asymmetrical power relationship and social dynamics. Empowering women puts the spotlight on education and employment which are an essential element to sustainable development.

Empowerment: Focus on poor women

In India, the trickle down effects of macro-economic policies have failed to resolve the problem of gender inequality. Women have been the vulnerable section of society and constitute a sizeable segment of the poverty-struck population. Women face gender specific barriers to access education, health, employment etc. Microfinance deals with women below the poverty line. Micro-loans are available solely and entirely to this target group of women. There are several reason for this: Among the poor, the poor women are most disadvantaged—they are characterized by lack of education and access of resources, both of which is required to help them work their way out of poverty and for upward economic and social mobility. The problem is more acute for women in countries like India, despite the fact that women's labour makes a critical contribution to the economy. This is due to the low social status and lack of access to key resources. Evidence shows that groups of women are better customers than men, the better managers of resources. If loans are routed through women, the benefits of loans are spread wider among the household.

Since women's empowerment is the key to socio-economic development of the community; bringing women into the mainstream of national development has been a major concern of government. The ministry of rural development has special components for women in its programmes. Funds are earmarked as "Women's component" to ensure flow of adequate resources for the same. Besides Swarnajayanti

Grameen Swarozgar Yojana (SGSY), Ministry of Rural Development is implementing other scheme having women's component .They are: Indira Awas Yojana (IAJ), National Social Assistance Programme (NSAP), Restructured Rural Sanitation Programme, Accelerated Rural Water Supply Programme (ARWSP) the (erstwhile) Integrated Rural Development Programme (IRDP), the (erstwhile) Development of Women and Children in Rural Areas (DWCRA) and the Jawahar Rozgar Yojana (JRY).

Concept and features of microfinance

The term microfinance is of recent origin and is commonly used in addressing issues related to poverty alleviation, financial support to micro-entrepreneurs, gender development etc. There is, however, no statutory definition of microfinance. The taskforce on Supportitative Policy and Regulatory Framework for Microfinance has defined microfinance as "Provision of thrift, credit and other financial services and products of very small amounts to the poor in rural, semi-urban or urban areas for enabling them to raise their income levels and improve living standards". The term "Micro" literally means "small". But the taskforce has not defined any amount. However as per Micro Credit Special Cell of the Reserve Bank of India, the borrowable amounts upto the limit of Rs. 25000 could be considered as micro-credit products and this amount could be gradually increased up to Rs. 40,000 over a period of time, which roughly equals to $500—a standard for South Asia as per international perceptions.

The term microfinance, sometimes is used inter-changeably with the term micro-credit. However while micro-credit refers to purveyance of loans in small quantities, the term microfinance has a broader meaning covering in its ambit other financial services like saving, insurance etc. as well.

The mantra "Microfinance" is banking through groups. The essential features of the approach are to provide financial services through the groups of individuals, formed either in joint liability or co-obligation mode. The other dimensions of the microfinance approach are:

- Savings/Thrift precedes credit
- Credit is linked with savings/thrift
- Absence of subsidies
- Group plays an important role in credit appraisal, monitoring and recovery.

Basically groups can be of two types:

Self-Help Groups (SHGs) : The group in this case does financial intermediation on behalf of the formal institution. This is the predominant model followed in India.

Grameen Groups: In this model, financial assistance is provided to the individual in a group by the formal institution on the strength of group's assurance. In other words, individual loans are provided on the strength of joint liability/ co-obligation. This microfinance model was initiated by Bangladesh Grameen Bank and is being used by some of the Microfinance Institutions (MFIs) in our country.

WOMEN'S EMPOWERMENT AND MICROFINANCE: DIFFERENT PARADIGMS

Concern with women's access to credit and assumptions about contributions to women's empowerment are not new. From the early 1970s women's movements in a number of countries became increasingly interested in the degree to which women were able to access poverty-focused credit programmes and credit cooperatives. In India organizations like Self-Employed Women's Association (SEWA) among others with origins and affiliations in the Indian labour and women's movements identified credit as a major constraint in their work with informal sector women workers.

The problem of women's access to credit was given particular emphasis at the first International Women's Conference in Mexico in 1975 as part of the emerging awareness of the importance of women's productive role both for national economies, and for women's rights. This led to the setting up of the Women's World Banking network and production of manuals for women's credit provision. Other women's organizations world-wide set up credit and savings components both as a way of increasing women's incomes and bringing women together to address wider gender issues. From the mid-1980s there was a mushrooming of donor, government and NGO-sponsored credit programmes in the wake of the 1985 Nairobi women's conference (Mayoux, 1995a).

The 1980s and 1990s also saw development and rapid expansion of large minimalist poverty-targeted microfinance institutions and networks like Grameen Bank, ACCION and Finca among others. In these organizations and others evidence of significantly higher female repayment rates led to increasing emphasis on targeting women as an efficiency strategy to increase credit recovery. A number of donors also saw female-targeted financially-sustainable microfinance as a means of marrying internal demands for increased efficiency because of declining budgets with demands of the increasingly vocal gender lobbies.

The trend was further reinforced by the Micro Credit Summit Campaign starting in 1997 which had 'reaching and empowering women' as its second key goal after poverty reduction (RESULTS, 1997). Microfinance for women has recently been seen as a key strategy in meeting not only Millennium Goal 3 on gender equality, but also Poverty Reduction, Health, HIV/AIDS and other goals.

Feminist Empowerment Paradigm

The feminist empowerment paradigm did not originate as a northern imposition, but is firmly rooted in the development of some of the earliest microfinance programmes in the south, including SEWA in India. It currently underlies the gender policies of many NGOs and the perspectives of some of the consultants and researchers looking at gender impact of microfinance programmes (e.g. Chen, 1996; Johnson, 1997).

Here the underlying concerns are gender equality and women's human rights. Women's empowerment is seen as an integral and inseparable part of a wider process of social transformation. The main target group is poor women and women capable of providing alternative female role models for change. Increasing attention has also been paid to men's role in challenging gender inequality.

Microfinance is promoted as an entry point in the context of a wider strategy for women's economic and socio-political empowerment which focuses on gender awareness and feminist organization. As developed by Chen in her proposals for a sub-sector approach to micro-credit, based partly on SEWA's strategy and promoted by UNIFEM, microfinance must be:

Part of a sectoral strategy for change which identifies opportunities, constraints and bottlenecks within industries which if addressed can raise returns and prospects for large numbers of women. Possible strategies include linking women to existing services and infrastructure, developing new technology such as labour-saving, food processing, building information networks, shifting to new markets, policy level changes to overcome legislative barriers and unionization.

Based on participatory principles to build up incremental knowledge of industries and enable women to develop their strategies for change (Chen, 1996). Economic empowerment is however defined in more than individualist terms to include issues such as property rights, changes in intra-household relations and transformation of the macro-economic context. Many organisations go further than interventions at the industry level to include gender-specific strategies for social and political empowerment. Some programmes have developed very effective means for integrating gender awareness into programmes and for organizing women and men to challenge and change gender discrimination. Some also have legal rights support for women and engage in gender advocacy. These interventions to increase social and political empowerment are seen as essential prerequisites for economic empowerment.

Poverty Reduction Paradigm

The poverty alleviation paradigm underlies many NGO integrated poverty-targeted community development programmes. Poverty alleviation here is defined in broader terms than market incomes to encompass increasing capacities and choices and decreasing the vulnerability of the poor people.

The main focus of programmes as a whole is on developing sustainable livelihoods, community development and social service provision like literacy, health care and infrastructure development. There is not only a concern with reaching the poor, but also the poorest.

Policy debates have focused particularly on the importance of small savings and loan provision for consumption as well as production, group formation and the possible justification for some level of subsidy for programmes working with particular client groups or in particular contexts. Some programmes have developed effective methodologies for poverty targeting and/or operating in remote areas. Such strategies have recently become a focus of interest from some donors and also the Micro Credit Summit Campaign.

Here gender lobbies have argued for targeting women because of higher levels of female poverty and women's responsibility for household well-being. However although gender inequality is recognised as an issue, the focus is on assistance to households and there is a tendency to see gender issues as cultural and hence not subject to outside intervention.

Although term 'empowerment' is frequently used in general terms, often synonymous with a multi-dimensional definition of poverty alleviation, the term 'women's empowerment' is often considered best avoided as being too controversial and political. The assumption is that increasing women's access to microfinance will enable women to make a greater contribution to household income and this, together with other interventions to increase household well-being, will translate into improved well-being for women and enable women to bring about wider changes in gender inequality.

Financial Sustainability Paradigm

The financial self-sustainability paradigm (also referred to as the financial systems approach or sustainability approach) underlies the models of microfinance promoted since the mid-1990s by most donor agencies and the Best Practice guidelines promoted in publications by USAID, World Bank, UNDP and CGAP.

The ultimate aim is on the programmes which are profitable and fully self-supporting in competition with other private sector banking institutions and able to raise funds from international financial markets rather than relying on funds from development agencies. The main target group, despite claims to reach the poorest, is the 'bankable poor': small entrepreneurs and farmers. This emphasis on financial sustainability is seen as necessary to create institutions which reach significant numbers of poor people in the context of declining aid budgets and opposition to welfare and redistribution in macro-economic policy.

Policy discussions have focused particularly on setting up of interest rates to cover costs, separation of microfinance from other interventions to enable separate accounting and programme expansion to increase outreach and economies of scale, reduction of transaction costs and ways of using groups to decrease costs of delivery. Recent guidelines for CGAP funding and best practice focus on production of a 'financial sustainability index' which charts progress of programmes in covering costs from incomes.

Within this paradigm gender lobbies have been able to argue for targeting women on the grounds of high female repayment rates and the need to stimulate women's economic activity as a hitherto underutilized resource for economic growth. They have had some success in ensuring that considerations of female targeting are integrated into conditions of microfinance delivery and programme evaluation.

Alongside this focus on female targeting, the term 'empowerment' is frequently used in promotional literature. Definitions of empowerment are in individualist terms with the ultimate aim being the expansion of individual choice or capacity for Self-reliance. It is assumed that increasing women's access to microfinance services will in itself lead to individual economic empowerment through enabling women's decisions about savings and credit use, enabling women to set up micro-enterprise, increasing incomes under their control. It is then assumed that this increased economic empowerment will lead to increased well-being of women and also to social and political empowerment.

These paradigms do not correspond systematically to any one organisational model of microfinance. Microfinance providers with the same organisational form, e.g. village bank, Grameen model or cooperative model may have very different gender policies and/or emphases and strategies for poverty alleviation. The three paradigms represent different 'discourses' each with its own relatively consistent internal logic in relating aims to policies, based on different underlying understandings of development. They are not only different, but often seen as 'incompatible discourses' in uneasy tension and with continually contested degrees of dominance. In many programmes and donor agencies there is considerable disagreement, lack of communication and/or personal animosity and promoted by different stakeholders within organisations between staff involved in microfinance (generally firm followers of financial self-sustainability), staff concerned with human development (generally with more sympathy for the poverty alleviation paradigm and emphasising participation and integrated development) gender lobbies (generally incorporating at least some elements of the feminist empowerment paradigm). What is of concern in current debates is the way in which the use of apparently similar terminology of empowerment, participation and sustainability conceals radical differences in policy priorities. Although women's empowerment may be a stated aim in the rhetoric of official gender policy and program promotion, in practice it becomes subsumed in and marginalised by concerns of financial sustainability and/or poverty alleviation.

MICROFINANCE INSTRUMENT FOR WOMEN'S EMPOWERMENT

Microfinance is emerging as a powerful instrument for poverty alleviation in the new economy. In India, microfinance scene is dominated by Self-Help Groups (SHGs)–Bank Linkage Programme, aimed at providing a cost-effective mechanism for providing financial services to the "unreached poor". Based on the philosophy of peer pressure and group savings as collateral substitute, the SHG programme has been successful in not only in meeting peculiar needs of the rural poor, but also in strengthening collective self-help capacities of the poor at the local level, leading to their empowerment.

Microfinance for the poor and women has received extensive recognition as a strategy for poverty reduction and for economic empowerment. Increasingly in the last five years, there is questioning of whether micro-credit is most effective approach to economic empowerment of poorest and, among them, women in particular. Development practitioners in India and developing countries often argue that the exaggerated focus on microfinance as a solution for the poor has led to neglect by the state and public institutions in addressing employment and livelihood needs of the poor.

Credit for empowerment is about organizing people, particularly around credit and building capacities to manage money. The focus is on getting the poor to mobilize their own funds, building their capacities and empowering them to leverage external credit. Perception of women is that learning to manage money and rotate funds builds women's capacities and confidence to intervene in local governance beyond the limited goals of ensuring access to credit. Further, it combines the goals of financial sustainability with that of creating community-owned institutions.

Before 1990s, credit schemes for rural women were almost negligible. The concept of women's credit was born on the insistence by women-oriented studies that highlighted the discrimination and struggle of women in having the access of credit. However, there is a perceptible gap in financing genuine credit needs of the poor especially women in the rural sector.

There are certain misconception about the poor people that they need loan at subsidized rate of interest on soft terms, they lack education, skill, capacity to save, credit worthiness and therefore are not bankable. Nevertheless, the experience of several SHGs reveal that rural poor are actually efficient managers of credit and finance. Availability of timely and adequate credit is essential for them to undertake any economic activity rather than credit subsidy.

The Government measures have attempted to help the poor by implementing different poverty alleviation programmes but with little success. Since most of them are target based involving lengthy procedures for loan disbursement, high transaction costs, and lack of supervision and monitoring. Since the credit requirements of the rural poor cannot be adopted on project lending approach as it is in the case of organized sector, there emerged the need for an informal credit supply through SHGs. The rural poor with the assistance from NGOs have demonstrated their potential for self help to secure economic and financial strength. Various case studies show that there is a positive correlation between credit availability and women's empowerment.

Problems and challenges

Surveys have shown that many elements contribute to make it more difficult for women empowerment through micro-businesses. These elements are:

- Lack of knowledge of the market and potential profitability, thus making the choice of business difficult.
- Inadequate book-keeping.
- Employment of too many relatives which increases social pressure to share benefits.
- Setting prices arbitrarily.
- Lack of capital.
- High interest rates.
- Inventory and inflation accounting is never undertaken.
- Credit policies that can gradually ruin their business

Other shortcoming includes.

Challenging economic empowerment

However impact on incomes is widely variable. Studies which consider income levels find that for the majority of borrowers income increases are small, and in some cases negative. All the evidence suggests that most women invest in existing activities which are low profit and insecure and/or in their husband's activities. In many programmes and contexts it is only in a minority of cases that women on their own can develop lucrative activities through credit and savings alone.

It is clear that women's choices about activity and their ability to increase incomes are seriously constrained by gender inequalities in access to other resources for investment, responsibility for household subsistence expenditure, lack of time because of unpaid domestic work and low levels of mobility, constraints on sexuality and sexual violence which limit access to markets in many cultures.

These gender constraints are in addition to market constraints on expansion of the informal sector and resource and skill constraints on the ability of poor men as well as women to move up from survival activities to expanding businesses. There are signs, particularly in some urban markets like Harare and Lusaka, that the rapid expansion of microfinance programmes may be contributing to market saturation in 'female' activities and hence declining profits.

Challenging social and political empowerment

There have been positive changes in household and community perceptions of women's productive role, as well as changes at the individual level. In societies like Sudan and Bangladesh where women's role has been very circumscribed and previously they had little opportunity to meet other women outside their immediate family there have sometimes been significant changes. It is likely that changes at the individual, household and community levels are interlinked and that individual women who gain respect in their households then act as role models for others leading to a wider process of change in community perceptions and male willingness to accept change (Lakshman, 1996).

Microfinance has also been strategically used by some NGOs as an entry point for wider social and political mobilisation of women around gender issues. For example, SEWA in India, CODEC in Bangladesh and CIPCRE in Cameroon, indicate the potential of microfinance to form a basis for organization against other issues like domestic violence, male alcohol abuse and dowry.

However there is no necessary link between women's individual economic empowerment and/or participation in microfinance groups and social and political empowerment. These changes are not an automatic consequence of microfinance *per se*. As noted above, women's increased productive role has also often had it costs.

In most programmes there is little attempt to link microfinance with wider social and political activity. In the absence of specific measures to encourage this there is little evidence of any significant contribution of microfinance. Microfinance groups may put severe strains on women's existing networks if repayment becomes a problem (Noponen, 1990; Rahman, 1999). There is evidence to the contrary that microfinance and income-earning may take women away from other social and political activities.

The evidence therefore indicates that contributions of microfinance *per se* to women's empowerment cannot be assumed and current complacency in this regard is misplaced. In many cases contextual constraints at all levels have prevented women from accessing programmes, increasing or controlling incomes or challenging subordination. Where women are not able to significantly increase incomes under their control or negotiate changes in intra-household and community gender inequalities, women may become dependent on loans to continue in very low-paid occupations with heavier workloads and enjoying little benefit.

For some women microfinance has been positively disempowering, as indicated by some of the cases shown above which are far from isolated examples:

- Credit (i.e. debt) may lead to severe impoverishment, abandonment and put serious strains on networks with other women.
- Pressure to save may mean women forgoing their own necessary consumption.
- The contribution of microfinance alone appears to be most limited for the poorest and most dis-advantaged women.

All the evidence suggests that the poorest women are the most likely to be explicitly excluded by programmes and also peer groups where repayment is the prime consideration and/or where the main emphasis of programmes is on existing micro-entrepreneurs. It also suggests that even where they get access to credit they are particularly vulnerable to falling further into debt.

Conclusions and suggestions

Numerous traditional and informal system of credit that were already in existence before microfinance came into vogue. Viability of microfinance needs to be understood from a dimension that is far broader in looking at its long-term aspects too. Very little attention has been given to empowerment questions or ways in which both empowerment and sustainability aims may be accommodated. Failure to take into account impact on income also has potentially adverse implications for both repayment and outreach, and hence also for financial sustainability. An effort is made here to present some of these aspects to complete the picture.

A conclusion that emerges from this account is that microfinance can contribute to solving the problems of inadequate housing and urban services as an integral part of poverty alleviation programmes. The challenge lies in finding the level of flexibility in the credit instrument that could make it match the multiple credit requirements of the low income borrower without imposing unbearably high cost of monitoring its end use upon the lenders. A promising solution is to provide multipurpose lone or composite credit for income generation, housing improvement and consumption support. Consumption loan is found to be especially important during the gestation period between commencing a new economic activity and deriving positive income. Careful research on demand for financing and savings behavior of the potential borrowers and their participation in determing the mix of multi-purpose loans are essential in making the concept work.

The organizations involved in micro-credit initiatives should take account of the fact that:

- Credit is important for development but cannot by itself enable very poor women to overcome their poverty.
- Making credit available to women does not automatically mean they have control over its use

and over any income they might generate from micro-enterprises.

- In situations of chronic poverty it is more important to provide saving services than to offer credit.
- A useful indicator of the tangible impact of micro-credit schemes is the number of additional proposals and demands presented by local villagers to public authorities.

Nevertheless ensuring that the microfinance sector continues to move forward in relation to gender equality and women's empowerment will require a long-term strategic process of the same order as the one in relation to poverty if gender is not to continue to 'evaporate' in a combination of complacency and resistance within donor agencies and the microfinance sector. This will involve:

- Ongoing exchange of experience and innovation between practitioners.
- Constant awareness and questioning of 'bad practice'.
- Lobbying donors for sufficient funding for empowerment strategies.
- Bringing together the different players in the sector to develop coherent policies and for gender advocacy.

India is the country where a collaborative model between banks, NGOs, MFIs and Women's organizations is furthest advanced. It therefore serves as a good starting point to look at what we know so far about 'Best Practice' in relation to microfinance for women's empowerment and how different institutions can work together.

It is clear that gender strategies in microfinance need to look beyond just increasing women's access to savings and credit and organizing self help groups to look strategically at how programmes can actively promote gender equality and women's empowerment. Moreover the focus should be on developing a diversified microfinance sector where different type of organizations—NGO, MFIs and formal sector banks all should have gender policies adapted to the needs of their particular target groups/institutional roles and capacities and collaborate and work together to make a significant contribution to gender equality and pro-poor development.

REFERENCES

1. Fisher, Thomas and M.S. Sriram (ed.), 2002, *Beyond Micro-credit: Putting Development Back into Microfinance*, New Delhi: Vistaar Publications; Oxford: Oxfam.
2. Harper, Malcolm, 2002, "Promotion of Self Help Groups under the SHG Bank Linkage Program in India", Paper presented at the Seminar on SHG-Bank Linkage Programme at New Delhi, November 25-26, 2002.
3. Kabeer, N., 2001, "Conflicts Over Credit: Re-evaluation the Empowerment Potential of Loans to Women in Rural Bangladesh": *World Development*, Vol. 29, No. 1.
4. Mayoux, L., 1998a. "Women's Empowerment and Microfinance programmes : Approaches, Evidence and Ways Forward." The Open University Working Paper No. 41.
5. Ackerley, B., 1995, Testing the Tools of Development: Credit Programmes , Loan Involvement and Women's Empowerment. World Development, 26(3), 56-68.

19

Impact of SHG Schemes on Women Empowerment in YSR (Kadapa) District

*Dr. Raghu Rama Murthi
**Dr. Rajani

Introduction

India is having more than 100 crores of population, women share equal in ratio having 496 million, that is 48 per cent to the population. The economic status of the women is generally poor which is a matter of great concern. The rural women directly or indirectly put their entrepreneurial skill in all rural employed activities such as agriculture operations, poultry, sheep rearing, dairy, sale of agricultural produce etc., though they put their heart and soul in rural employment activities, their economic status is not improved. Even though they have entrepreneurial skills, due to poor financial strength they need financial assistance. Hence, the need for designing exclusive self-employment and other developmental programmes for promotion of women entrepreneurship was greatly stressed.

The government has been implementing various programmes to provide self-employment opportunities to un-

* Department of Political Science, Government Degree College for Men, Anatapur.

** Academic Consultant, Department of Commerce, Yogi Vemana University, Kadapa-516003

employed including women. Among them Self-Help Groups (SHGs) playing a significant role. The SHG growth, which has almost assumed the form of a movement, represents a massive grassroots level mobilization of poor rural women to small informal associations capable of forging links with formal systems to help access financial and other services needed for their socio-economic advancement. Basically, SHGs are being promoted as a part of the microfinance interventions aimed at helping the poor to obtain easily financial services like savings, credit and insurance.

Self-Help Groups (SHGs): An overview

The promotion of SHGs in India begun more formally in 1992 with the launch of the SHG-Bank Linkage Programme by National Bank for Agricultural and Rural Development (NABARD). The main aim of the programme is to improve rural poors' access to formal credit system in a cost-effective sustainable manner by making use of SHGs which cover all economically viable activities including agriculture and allied activities. The normal bank rate of interest shall be charged, it may be between 9 to 11 per cent. On 1st July 2004, 0.25 paise interest rate came into existence.

Rationale of the study

Keeping in view the significance of SHGs in augmenting the entrepreneurial skills among women, the present study has been undertaken to evaluate the implementation of SHGs scheme in Kadapa district, a drought-prone and backward district in the state of Andhra Pradesh. The study is confined to the woman beneficiaries. Secondary data with regard to status in number of beneficiaries, social strata and bank linkage are collected from the authentic records of the DRDA, Kadapa. In addition, field study has been conducted to collect primary data with regard to the problems of women beneficiaries through pre-tested schedules.

Status of SHGs

Table 19.1 discloses the details with regard to number of groups formed from 2004-05 to 2007-08.

Table 19.1: Year-wise status of SHGs formed in Kadapa district

Year	No. of groups cumulative since inception	New groups
2004-05	18,000	—
2005-06	24,600	6600
2006-07	28,455	3855
2007-08*	32,610	4155

*Upto 9th Sept 2007.

Source: Figures compiled from the records of DRDA, Kadapa.

It is observed that the number of women beneficiaries under SHGs increased from 18,000 in 2004-05 to 32,610 during 2007-08, constituting more than 80 per cent growth rate. However, the year-wise growth rate is sluggish.

Social status

Table 19.2 reflects the caste-wise details of women SHGs.

It is evident from the table 19.2 that majority of the women beneficiaries belong to O.C. category followed by B.C. category. Minorities are very low because of existence of various social problems. The downtrodden and retarded sections like SC and ST are fewer in number. This may be due to un-favourble economic, political, social and administrative conditions.

Bank Linkage Programme

Under this scheme loans are deployed to women beneficiaries by banks on the recommendation of DRDA authorities. Table 19.3 manifests the number of women SHGs and loans sanctioned to them from 2004-05 to 2007-08.

Table 19.2: Caste-wise classification of women beneficiaries

Caste	2004-05	2005-06	2006-07	2007-08
O.C.	6254 (34.74)	8215 (33.39)	9870 (34.68)	10960 (33.61)
B.C.	5925 (32.92)	7820 (31.79)	9012 (31.67)	10497 (32.19)
S.C.	3423 (19.02)	4975 (20.02)	6841 (24.04)	7396 (22.68)
S.T.	612 (3.4)	842 (3.42)	862 (3.29)	7396 (22.68)
Minorities	1786 (9.92)	2798 (11.38)	1870 (6.32)	2854 (8.75)
Total	**18000 (100)**	**24600 (100)**	**28455 (100)**	**32610 (100)**

Source: Same as in Table 19.1.
Note : Figures in parentheses represent percentage to total.

Table 19.3: Coverage of SHGs and the amount sanctioned by various banks in Kadapa district

(Rs. in lakhs)

Year	No. of SHGs	Amount sanctioned
2004-05	5426	3142
2005-06	10600	7245
2006-07	12526	10274
2007-08*	5965	8094

*Upto 5th Sept. 08.
Source: Same as in table 19.1.

The number of SHGs under bank linkage programme increased from 5426 in 2004-05 to 12526 in 2006-07 and 5965 SHGs have been covered upto 5th September, 2008. It is expected that this number would go up by 13,000 by the end of December, 2008.

Bank-wise break up

The credit deployment by banks to SHGs has registered an

increasing trend. During the year 2004-05, an amount of Rs. 3142 lakhs was sanctioned by various banks in the district, which substantially rose to Rs. 10,274 lakhs by the end of 2006-07. A considerable amount, i.e. Rs. 8,094 was sanctioned by the banks upto 5th September, 2008. It is expected that this amount would increase by Rs. 14,000 lakhs by the end of the year 2007-08. Table 19.4 depicts the bank-wise participation in financing SHGs in the district.

Table 19.4: Amount sanctioned by banks to SHGs

(Rs. in lakhs)

Sl. No.	Name of the Bank	2004-05	2005-06	2006-07	2007-08
1.	Andhra Bank	125.09	276.04	350.07	239.61
2.	Central Bank of India	50.00	0.40	85.00	—
3.	Canara Bank	0.70	0.14	0.90	—
4.	Corporation Bank	29.11	83.26	118.15	142.34
5.	Indian Bank	0.15	7.00	5.00	—
6.	Punjab National Bank	50.00	1.75	0.31	—
7.	Andhra Pragathi Grameena Bank	1839.13	4472.87	5821.09	4452.54
8.	State Bank of Hyderabad	2.76	3.17	4.96	6.02
9.	State Bank of India	677.41	1701.64	2660.80	2446.85
10.	Syndicate Bank	356.73	683.26	1187.17	723.48
11.	Union Bank of India	4.80	7.70	14.55	4.80
12.	The Ing Vysba Bank	6.75	8.20	23.25	78.11
	Total	**3142.63**	**7245.43**	**10274.06**	**8094.08**

It is evidenced from table 19.4 that Andhra Pragathi Grameena Bank captured first place among all banks in credit deployment to the SHGs and followed by State Bank of India and Syndicate Bank. As a rural bank, AGB has been instrumental for developing women entrepreneurs by providing adequate credit.

Impediments/Challenges of women entrepreneurs

In order to identify the major problems encountered by women entrepreneurs of SHGs, 75 women beneficiaries have been selected at random. The selection is based on the list of women beneficiaries supplied by DRDA, Kadapa. Table 19.5 focuses on the major problems encountered by the sample respondents. Almost all the respondents reported multiple problems.

Table 19.5: Problems reported by women SHGs

Sl. No.	Problems	No. of respondents	% to total*
1.	Personal problems	43	57
2.	Education problems	33	44
3.	Social problems	30	40
4.	Economic/Financial problems	50	67
5.	Technological problems	25	33
6.	Raw material problems	35	47
7.	Marketing problems	55	73
8.	Manpower support problems	30	40
9.	Competition from large firms	38	51
10.	Bureaucratic delay in getting payments from government departments	35	47

*Multiple Responses

Source: Field survey

It is apparent from table 19.5 that large numbers of respondents (55) have reported marketing as a major problem. Next to marketing, financial problems have been reported by 50 respondents, constituting 67 per cent of the sample size. The rest of the respondents complained competition from personal, large firms, social disparities etc., as other major problems seriously affecting their units.

Conclusion

To conclude, the awareness in rural areas among women belong to weaker sections is still limited. In addition, a major area of difficulty for women entrepreneur is that of marketing. Hence, strategies should be formulated to inculcate marketing skills and to enable the women entrepreneurs to sell their products with ease. The government has to make efforts for providing marketing facilities by opening various marketing stalls and exhibitions etc. Another major problem on part of women entrepreneurs is restrictive loan policies of the banks. The banks took long time to clearly recognize and internalize the concept. Some of the banks in the district were forcing the beneficiaries to pledge properties as collateral securities.

Majority of the women beneficiaries are not completely aware of the procedure of SHG scheme. The DRDA and banks have to conduct awareness programmes to improve awareness among rural women. SHG members have often lacked business skills and administrative capacity due to the inadequate provision of education and training. So, the government organs like DRDA and banks have to provide training facilities. In this regard, the non-government organizations and other associations should take initiative to make the women aware and motivate them towards self-employment. Further, women should be encouraged to start ventures confidently with enthusiasm by employing modern technology. They have to shift their line of activities on scientific and modern lines. The government should ensure a speedy change from traditional occupation to modern business enterprises in order to take the maximum benefit of new market conditions and technology. These measures, no doubt would certainly change traditional women and mould them as omnipotent.

REFERENCES

- *Economic Times*, New Delhi Edition, 29 August, 2005.
- Ajaha, R.K., Self Help Groups and Rural Employment, *Yojana*, April, 2001.
- Note on self-employment schemes in Kadapa District, DRDA, Kadapa.
- Mahajan, V. et al. (1999) Dhakka starting microfinance in India Chapter 29 in *Microfinance Emerging Challenges* (eds) K. Basu and K. Jindal, Tata McGraw, New Delhi.
- Satya Sundaram, I., *Rural Development*, Himalaya Publishing House, New Delhi, 2002.

Index

D

E

F

G

H

I

J

K

L

M

R

S

Y

Z